What's Cooking
in the
Cotswolds

by

Angela Hewitt

Travelling
Gourmet
Publications

Travelling Gourmet Publications:

Cooking on the Move
A cookery book for caravanners, campavanners and boaters cooking in a
confined mobile kitchen. Price: 4.50

What's Cooking in the New Forest. Second edition. Price 4.95

What's Cooking on the Isle of Wight. Second edition. Price 4.75

What's Cooking in the Cotswolds. Price 4.95

What's Cooking in and Around Brighton. Price 4.95

What's Cooking in and Around Oxford. Price 4.95

*The Herb Growers Recipe Book
and Directory of Herb Specialists.* Price 3.45

*Taste of Herbs
- Lavender - Mint - Elderflowers - Parsley - Tarragon - Basil -*
A gift pack containing a sachet of herbs complete with 7 delicious recipes.
Price 2.25 each.   Mixed Pack of 6. Price 6.95.

Published by: Travelling Gourmet Publications
Padmore Lodge, Beatrice Avenue
East Cowes, Isle of Wight

Written, designed and illustrated by: Angela Hewitt
Copy Right: What's Cooking Series: Travelling Gourmet Publications
Printed and bound in England by: Itchen Printers ltd.

Recommended Price £4.95

What's Cooking in the Cotswolds

in the

Cotswolds

*Recipes from many Restaurants, Cafes,
Tearooms, Pubs, Producers and Suppliers
in the Cotswolds*

*The definitive guide to cooking,
shopping and eating out.*

This book is dedicated
to all those who believe small is beautiful, and to all
those individual food and catering businesses who
dedicate their lives to personally providing only the
best in food and service.

And to all of you; tourists and locals alike, who
support these businesses and by doing so keep our
unique heritage alive.

Contents

Cooking Notes

Oven Temperatures Vary particularly in fan ovens which can be hotter and should be reduced a notch. Old ovens can also vary. The temperatures in this book are only a guide to what the optimum oven should be.

Measurements should not be mixed. Stick to one or the other, imperial or metric.

Baking Blind means to line an uncooked pastry case with greaseproof paper or tin foil then fill with dried beans. This acts as a weight and prevents the pastry from rising in the centre and collapsing around the side during baking. The case should be cooked in a hot oven for 15-20 minutes or until the pastry is cooked and a pale golden colour.

Pastry is sometimes called for in a recipe without giving precise instructions. if 8oz-225gm of pastry is required, this means pastry made with 8oz-225gm of plain flour. If using ready made pastry then 12oz-350gm is usually required.

Bain Marie or Water Bath, is a large roasting pan or saucepan filled with hot water in which a smaller dish or basin containing the food is placed. The idea is to keep a difficult sauce i.e bernaise, warm, or to protect the sides of something delicate while it is being cooked in the oven, for instance a baked egg custard.

Introduction

Despite modern pressures the Cotswolds still manages to maintain its country village charm. There is a strong tradition of farming steeped in a fascinating history, and much of it survives today albeit in a reduced and cottage-industry form.

The food and cooking in the Cotswolds strongly reflects the produce of the region. It's cheeses, orchard fruits, freshwater fish, and rare breed animals are only a few of what is available. Much is done to encourage the use of regional foods. For instance the Taste of Glorious Gloucester Competition which is open to amateur and professional cooks has now become a well supported event. I couldn't help but notice how seriously everyone took their cooking, how much care they put into every dish and how proud they were to be using so much local produce when creating a new recipe.

The recipes in this book, contributed by local cooks and producers show a strong sense of the area. Everyone has put a lot of trouble into writing them in between their very busy work schedule, some have even given away a few secrets.

The locals are very lucky to have such an excellent choice of places to eat out and of specialist shops that provide such wonderful produce. Tourists to the area will also quickly discover how lucky they are, when wandering through country towns and villages to find delicious refreshments to keep them going.

Tourism is growing in the Cotswolds and the standard of cooking is growing too. Disciples of the many 'Good' food guides will already be aware of this. It won't be long before it is considered, as is the Lake District, one of England's gourmet centres. To my mind it already is.

Restaurant Law. When you make a reservation, even by phone, you are entering a legal contract. If for some reason you are unable to keep that reservation please let them know. No matter how short the notice. At least you are giving them a chance to resell the table to a casual caller. Failure to do so could incur a cancellation fee. So, don't spoil your holiday, please let them know.

The Cotswolds

Its name alone tells a story, 'Cot' means ancient enclosure for sheep and 'Wold' means the rolling hills. This name can still perfectly describe the area. The sheep are less but nevertheless still around and the hills are as beautiful as ever. They cover an area of 790 square miles which runs into six counties; Gloucestershire enjoying the lions share. Most of this area has now been designated an area of outstanding natural beauty.

Today the Cotswolds is renowned for its soft honey coloured stone walls and buildings. Designs have changed through the ages, but from when the first cottage was built before the arrival of the Romans out of the areas indigenous stone right up to today, the same stone has been used. It remained untouched by the surge of the industrial revolution and it was then as it still is now considered an away-from-it-all- place. A sanctuary and an idyllic example of English country life.

For the tourist and local population rural interests are diverse. From the pleasures of the river Severn and the smaller rivers that run throughout the Cotswolds valleys, that offer water sports, fishing and river bank picnics, to the ancient tracks that ran between early settlements providing miles of winding paths for the rambler.

The Cotswolds is brimming with interest for anyone keen on architecture and old churches and the history is rich from its many customs celebrated by festivals throughout the year to its deeply steeped farming and agriculture which played a part in the subtle development of the landscape. Going further into the past we have an archaeologists fun fair. Here he will find hill forts, Roman villas, and many stone age long barrows where he can dream about the past.

Endless days and hours can be spent idlly wondering through the many tiny villages that form the pattern of the Cotswolds. Some are so small they are lost between the undulating vales. Cotswold stone is a major feature and give a picture book charm as thrilling as any picturesque village in Europe.

Here is a part of Little England that remains relatively untouched. Much of which is thanks to the industrial revolution that drew people away from the villages and into the towns in the search of more fruitful work.

Today its charm is being rediscovered, small villages and community's are no longer collapsing.People eager to escape city life are returning, tourists are taking an interest in this unspoilt area. To feed the tourists hunger,small craft industries are re-emerging as are pubs, cafes, restaurants and hotels. All this will increase the wealth of the area, which will in turn help, under the strict controls of the local councils, to preserve the character of village life.

The Cotswold Way

In a era of keeping fit but with a gentler,less aggressive exercise routine, this ten days, 100 mile walk has become a major attraction to the Cotswolds.

Most people will have little idea of how much effort has gone into developing the Cotswold Way. If it had been the resurrection of an ancient rout things might have been easier, but it is in fact the linking together of a series of existing rights of way. The links were not easy to achieve and in some cases years of negotiation, and treading carefully, were needed to get permission from landowners to let the Way cross their land. Most landowners saw the advantage of this as walkers would be kept on the straight and narrow and not be left to wander aimlessly and sometimes indiscriminately over the land.

The walk was originally conceived in 1950 by the Gloucestershire ramblers association; but never came to fruition until 1970, the year of the National Footpath Week.

In 1975 operation Cotswaymark was launched. Waymarking (yellow arrows, now a national walkers symbol) now marks the entire route. For the explorer who likes that 'first discovered' feel, waymarking is a bit of a dampner, but for the majority of walkers it makes them feel comfortable to know they are walking on legitimate ground.

The original concept of the Cotswold Way was to walk from north to south. However, the predominant south-west winds rendered this a little uncomfortable; so, it is recommended that walkers start off from Bath walking towards the north with the wind, rain and sun on their back. Don't forget to take a picnic, perhaps prepared by the local delicatessen and some elderflower cordial for a refreshing drink from the Bottle Green company.

Cotswold Country Code

Take nothing but a photograph
Leave nothing but footprints
Kill nothing but time

Starters

As a prelude to a larger meal a starter should be small, light and appetizing. Something to whet the appetite and stimulate the gastric juices.

Many of the starters in this section can be served as a light snack or lunch by increasing the proportions and accompanying with a crisp, lightly dressed salad and freshly baked bread.

When choosing your starter, most important of all is a question of balance. For instance, avoid serving two cream based dishes together, and if you are serving two fish dishes try and make one of them shell fish.

For ease, soup is by far the best option. It can be prepared in advance then re-heated at the last minute. If soup is to be hot make sure it is piping and if cold it should be icy cold.

Whatever your choice, remember a starter is not to be made a meal of, and the emphasis should be on "little and light".

Jenny Wren's Wholesome Vegetable Soup

A hearty soup for a large party.

1lb-450gm onions, chopped
3 leeks, chopped
1lb-450gm carrots
1lb-450gm potatoes, peeled and chopped
1 small cauliflower, cut into florets
1 bunch cress
2 large swede, chopped
2 tins mushy peas
8oz-225gm margarine
8oz-225gm plain flour
1 tspn mixed herbs, 1 sachet bouquet garni
1 tspn celery salt, 1 tspn garlic powder
1 tspn veg bullion mix
salt and pepper

1...In a large saucepan place all the chopped vegetables with the exception of the onions. Add water to cover, cover with a lid and boil until the vegetables are soft.
2...Melt the margarine in another saucepan and add the chopped onions, mixed herbs, garlic powder and celery salt. Cook until the onions are soft.
3...Remove from the heat and fold in the plain flour and add the two tins of mushy peas.
4...Strain the vegetables (retain the water) then mash the vegetables.
5...Mix the vegetable bouillon with 1pt-570ml of the reserved vegetable water and add to the flour mixture.
6...Gradually add the mashed vegetables and the rest of the water to the flour mixture. Bring to the boil. Chop the cress and add to the soup then add the sachet of bouquet garni. Simmer for 10 minutes. Add extra water if too thick. Remove the bouquet garni and serve with crusty bread.
Ideal for freezing.
From the kitchen of...

THE JENNY WREN
11 The Street, Bibury, Cirencester, Glos   Tel: 01285 740555
Proprietors: Mr J Kemp
Chefs: Mrs M Chivers
Open: All year Winter 10am - 4pm. Summer 10am-5.30pm. Closed 1 week Christmas.
Casual callers and children welcome. Wheelchair access. Bed & Breakfast. Licensed.
Outside seating in teagarden. Traditional home-cooking. Vegetarian dishes. Full menu all day.

The Shopping Basket

It is a sad fact that if we don't support our local shops and small producers they will disappear without trace.

The convenience of the supermarket has beguiled us all and yet their fresh produce such as meat, vegetables and bread, food we would normally have bought from the butcher, the baker and the green grocer, is more expensive to buy at the supermarket.

An important area where the supermarket falls down is in its disinterest in promoting local produce; for example speciality ice creams, chocolates, biscuits, chutneys etc. Thanks to the local delicatessen, specialist producers of Britains regional food can at least find readily available shelf space to promote their goods.

The Cotswolds is rich in specialist shops, it would be difficult to find another area with a better bounty.

Small gourmet shops, such as Gastromania run by a dedicated connoisseur, are stuffed with a huge range of international as well as regional foods. Many of these shops offer an invaluable service of ready prepared meals for the customer who wants to eat well but have little time or inclination to cook.

For the keen cook, Tetbury Traditional Meats offer organic meat, much of it derived from rare breeds farmers, cut and trimmed just how you like it. Sausages are in many places sold as luxury items made to special recipes at Tetbury meats as well as the Sausage Company.

Fresh local fish such as wild salmon, the famous elvers, eels and other freshwater and estuary caught fish are abundant i when in season. If you prefer a good rainbow trout pop round to Ruskin Mill where trout are raised in their mill pond. While there stock up with fresh organic vegetables and herbs.

Local apples are a must, especially if they are served with the local rare breed of Gloucester Old Spot or for afters in a delicious English apple pie.

If you are a rambler then gather together a meal of local cheese, double Gloucester, single Gloucester or Cerney goats cheese with some delicious locally baked bread and an apple from the House of Cheese in Tetbury. For a healthy option pick up a home-made pie from Bomfords delicatessen in Cirencester.

To keep this bounty of produce alive it is essential that we support our small local shops and producers. The small shopkeeper is part of our National Heritage. Apart from that we desperately need them and the competition they give the big boys. If they are forced to close through lack of business it is inevitable that supermarkets will have a monopoly and general food prices will climb sky high and choice will be reduced in the name of profits.

When you are on holiday with more time on your hands, and a slower pace to your schedule, you can find the time to search out these small shops and enjoy the traditional pleasures of being served all that delicious local food. There's no shadow of a doubt it has been prepared with loving care, not for the masses but for you, the individual.

Great Britain has some of the best food in the world and the most humanely produced. Don't let anyone tell you otherwise.

Split Pea and Potato Soup

This soup is a real Winter warmer.

12oz-350gm onions, chopped
2 tbls olive oil
5pts-2.8lt good flavoured beef stock
8oz-225gm dried yellow split peas
2lb-900gm King Edward potatoes, peeled and diced
1 tspn freshly ground black pepper
½ tspn salt

1…Sweat down the onions in the olive oil for about 10 minutes until soft but not brown.
2…Add the stock and bring to the boil.
3…Add the split peas and potatoes. Simmer for 40 minutes.
4…Add the seasoning. Blend thoroughly using a hand held blender until the soup is completely smooth. Serve with chunky bread or a granary roll.

Note: If you do not wish to make such a large quantity, you can scale down the recipe to suit your needs.However this heart-warming soup freezes beautifully an is an excellent stand-by for all occasions.

From the kitchen of…

CHANCELLORS AT PAINSWICK
Kingsley House, Victoria Street, Painswick, Glos GL6 6QA.   Tel:01425 812451 Fax: 814258
Proprietor: Al Menzies and James Prince
Chef: James Prince
Open: Mon-Sat 10.30am-5pm. Sunday 12noon-5pm. Winter closed Wednesday. Summer open 7 days.
Closed Christmas.
Casual callers and children welcome. Separate room for smokers.
All cakes, scones, soups and specials are home-made. Sandwiches and snacks are freshly made to order. Vegetarian dishes.

Rolling the Gloucester

Whit Monday in the Cotswolds is an important day for cheese. This is the day when the annual custom of cheese-rolling down Coopers Hill. This is the most famous of all the customs that appear to surround Gloucester cheese. The reason for the rise of this custom seems unknown but speculation suggests that the cheeses were wheel shaped and hard crusted.

Gloucester cheese has a long history. and was made as far back as the eight century. Gloucester cheese is still made today but not in the large quantities of the past. Its character has also changed in as much as original Gloucester was made with the milk from the now almost extinct Gloucester Cow.

Gloucester cattle are an ancient breed similar in look to the wild ox. It is a relatively native breed and possibly a descendant of a Norwegian breed which was imported from Normandy in the 11th century. A handsome beast, it has a and black head and legs, a rich chestnut hide and a sharp profile with large white upswept horns. It is larger than the Guernsey and smaller than the Ayrshire. Along with the excellent grazing produced by the rich soil of the Vales and the large percentage of fat of small-globulin size in the milk the Gloucester was perfect for cheese-making and gave the Gloucester cheeses, both single and double their distinctiveness. Gloucester cheese is mentioned by name as early as 1595. Sadly, in the late 18th century disease hit the herds and they were replaced by Longhorns from the Midlands.

The difference between Double and Single Gloucester is in the cream content. Recipes have changed over the centuries but generally speaking Single Gloucester is made from skimmed evening milk, ripened overnight then added to full-cream morning milk. Having less fat they are a smaller cheese and normally eaten younger than Double Gloucester. Double Gloucester is made from the overnight cream or ripened, overnight whole milk (in 1772) added to the morning milk.

Double Gloucester was popular for many years and held a good price. it was even exported to America. No one knows the real reason for the decline in the traditional Gloucester cheese. A variety of reasons from the decline of the herds that gave it its distinctive flavour, to the growing competition from other cheese areas which in turn created efforts to reduce their own prices and inevitably their quality.

In 1974 Charles and Monica Martell re-formed the Gloucester Cattle Society and built up a healthy herd from a mere surviving forty five. In 1979 the national total passed the one hundred mark.

Today Smart's Gloucester Cheeses produces both Double and Single Gloucester Cheese from unpasteurized milk from her herd of Holsteins.

Warm Watercress Tartlets with Double Gloucester Sauce

A elegant starter which can also be served as a vegetarian luncheon dish.

1 bunch bright green watercress
1 medium potato, peeled and cooked
1 small onion
2 large eggs
½pt double cream
salt and pepper
pinch freshly grated nutmeg
8oz-225gm short pastry made with: 8oz-225gm plain flour, 3oz-75gm
butter, 2oz-50gm lard, 1 small egg.
double Gloucester sauce
4oz-110gm double Gloucester cheese
¼pt-150gm white wine
¼pt-150ml stock
8fl oz-200ml double cream
pepper, pinch freshly grated nutmeg

1...Make the pastry. Chill in the fridge for at least 20 minutes before using.
Divide the pastry into four pieces and roll out each portion into a circle
large enough to line a small 3" quiche tin. Bake blind in a pre-heated oven
200c/400f.gas6 for 15 minutes or until pale and golden.
2...Wash the watercress and remove any 'woody' stems. Roughly chop and
put in an enamel or stainless steel saucepan with the onion and the potato.
Add a drop of oil. Cover tightly and steam over a very low heat until the
watercress has wilted.
3...Tip into a blender and add the two eggs, the ½pt of double cream and
seasoning. Blend until smooth.
4...Spoon the mixture into the pre-cooked pastry cases and return to the
oven. 190c/375f/gas5 for about 30 minutes or until the watercress mixture
is set.
5...Keep warm while you make the sauce: Put the white wine and stock in a
saucepan and reduce by half. Lower the temperature. Grate the Gloucester
cheese and add to the white wine. Cook gently until the cheese has melted.
Add the cream and bring to the boil. Add seasoning.
6...Remove the tartlets from their rings and place on warm plates. Garnish
with a small bouquet of leaves and a few green grapes and pour around the
sauce.

William Pear Stuffed with North Cerney Goats Cheese

Tracey Price entered this recipe for the 'Glorious Gloucester Recipe and Cooking Competition'.

4 William pears
8oz-225gm North Cerney goats cheese
6oz-175gm lollo rosso
6oz-175gm curly endive
4oz-110gm walnuts
4oz-110gm chives

1...Peel the pears and remove the core from the base of the pear with a teaspoon or small sharp pointed knife to form a hollow. Poach in simmering water for about 5 minutes.
2...Stuff the pear with the North Cerney goats cheese and bake in a medium hot oven for a further 5 minutes.
3...Break the salad leaves into small pieces, wash and mix together with the walnut halves.
4...Place a small amount of salad on plates then place the pear in the middle.
5...Sprinkle chopped chives around the outside of the dish.

From the kitchen of...

THE CLOSE HOTEL
and Restaurant
Long Street, Tetbury, Glos GL8 8AQ.   Tel:01666 502272
Proprietors: Passport Hotels ltd
Managed by: Virgin Hotels ltd
Chef: Paul Welch and team
Open: All year
Uses fresh local ingredients that promotes regional dishes and produce.

Hot Tomato Tart

As well as making her own bread, Judy often uses a brioche dough as an alternative to conventional pastry.

This is a late Summer or early Autumn dish when tomatoes are at their best. There is no point in making this dish with imported, out-of-season, tasteless tomatoes. Judy has a wonderful source of supply in Smart's nursery at Shurdington just two miles from their restaurant. Their tomatoes bring back childhood memories of tomatoes picked and eaten in the garden.

Brioche pastry:
10oz-275gm plain or strong flour
4fl oz-100ml milk
½oz-10gm fresh yeast
½ tspn sugar
2oz-50gm Krona or margarine
2 eggs
salt
Filling:
11 medium sized tomatoes (1 per tart + 3)
salt and pepper
basil laves
2 egg yolks

1...First make the brioche pastry: Mash together the sugar and yeast. Add the milk and eggs and beat lightly together.
2...Put the flour and fat in your blender and mix. Add the yeast mixture and beat for a minute or so.
3...Tip out the dough into a lightly oiled plastic bag (do not seal it) and leave in a warm place. When it is well risen put in the fridge for at least 4 hours. After this time it will have the texture of soft pastry and can be easily rolled out and cut. This mixture makes 8 small tarts or one very large one. NB. This pastry needs to be made some hours in advance, but once made will keep in the fridge for a couple of days.
4...Make the filling: Peel all of the tomatoes and slice 8 of them thinly. Sprinkle with salt, pepper and basil (they can be left a couple of hours at this point).
5...Put the 'three' tomatoes in a blender with the egg yolks and liquidise.
6...To assemble the tarts; Roll out the pastry and line 8 individual or 1 large tart tin.

7...Pile the sliced tomatoes into the brioche cases. Sprinkle with more basil. Pour on the liquidised tomato mixture.

8...Bake in a hot pre-heated oven 200c/400f/gas6 for 2 minutes. Serve with a cucumber salad dressed with a herb vinaigrette.

From the menu of...

KINGSHEAD HOUSE RESTAURANT
Birdlip, Gloucestershire GL4 8JH.   Tel: 01452 862299
Proprietors: Judy and Warren Knock
Chef: Judy Knock
Open: All year. Evening Tues-Sat 7.30-10pm Lunch Tues-Fri and Sunday 12.15-2pm. Closed 25/26/27Dec.
Booking advised but casual callers welcome if there's room. Children welcome. Credit cards accepted. Outside seating in the Summer.
Twice weekly changing menu featuring hot rabbit paté in brioche and pear and prune galette with walnuts. Vegetarian dishes. Uses the freshest and best of local ingredients.

Salads for all Seasons

Capable of vast diversification, a salad can be sweet or savoury, or both, and can encapsulate as many ingredients as you can imagine. It's only criteria - until now - is that it should be cold. Nowadays it is extremely smart to serve salads warm.

The most sprightly of foods, a salad smells of freshness and astringent green. It can be crisp and dry or soft and juicy; coated in a translucent veil or a creamy mask. It can be raw or cooked or a fusion of the two. Like a musical score a salad is composed.

It may a simple mix or a sophisticated compilation of many parts. But whether simply green or a grand salmagundi, it should be attractive to the eye and full of life with fresh vibrant colours glistening with health.

Deceptively, salad takes time to prepare. The washing and shaking, the slicing and shredding and then the slow but therapeutic liaison of oil and eggs, is all time consuming. Such effort may seem futile with hungry mouths to feed; but, nicest of all, salad takes time to eat. The slow munching and crunching of ones labours brings a far more appreciable end to a meal. More than anything it is nice to see a salad linger at the table, to be dipped into at any time, even after the pudding.

Traditionally the British served salad as a main meal for lunch or tea. it was a very basic 'Famous Five' event, with cold ham (very good cold ham), boiled eggs, lettuce, tomato, cucumber, spring onions, beetroot and salad cream.

Even when the Continentals introduced us to the idea of serving a side salad with our steak and chips, it was still only very basic. If a chef dared to introduce a few sliced peppers he was complemented with great gusto.

These days we see a dramatic change on restaurant menus. Salad is now listed as an elegant starter rather than an added extra at the bottom of the page.

In the mid-late 1980's the Italians and Californians had a major influence on our cuisine. The Italians gave us vintage olive oil with characteristics that ranged from peppery to fruity, from mellow to acidic and a dedicated salad maker would have more than one variety in her store cupboard along with her French nut oils given to us in the late 70's and early 80's.

The Californians on the other hand gave us, char grilling and smoky favours. Although not for the first time. They originally gave us the barbecue, but this time around we can do it indoors rather than wait for a burst of Summer sun.

Salad is no longer warm weather food. Winter salads are equally as popular albeit quite different. Lettuce is more coarse and bitter such as radichio and frisse, and salad vegetables tend to come from under the ground, i.e leeks, celeriac and, Jerusalem artichokes. Meat additions are invariably gamy- and everyone should take seasonal advantage of pigeon, mallard, partridge and pheasant. Choice of seasonal fruit is limited to apples and pears and citrus varieties. Other fruits can be bought but they are often at out of season prices. Some ingredients such as avocado, aubergine, capsicum, oranges, nuts, beetroot, salmon, chicken livers, charcuterie and cheeses are available through out the year. But whatever the season, whether it is the plentiful Summer or the more Spartan Winter a lively salad can always be conjured.

Casserole of Artichokes and Asparagus in a Cider Butter Sauce

A delicious dish incorporating two of the finest ingredients available, with an invigorating sauce. Ideal as a starter served with warm brioche. For non-vegetarians, add some diced smoked bacon.

6 small artichoke bottoms (if not fresh, tinned) cut into quarters
1lb-450gm asparagus, cooked and cut into 2"-5cm pieces
2oz-50gm butter
10oz-275gm finely chopped shallots
4oz-110gm diced bacon, optional
2fl oz-50ml dry white wine
2fl oz-50ml cider
¼pt-150ml vegetable stock
2 small tomatoes, seeded and roughly chopped
2 sprigs of fresh basil
1 tbls double cream

1...In a small saucepan melt down a little of the butter and sweat the shallots by allowing them to cook without colouring.
2... Add the artichoke hearts and then the white wine and cider. Reduce by half and then add the vegetable stock. Cook for a further 5 minutes.
3...Remove the artichokes and reduce the liquid by half again.
4...Once the juice is at the required consistency, add the asparagus and artichokes.
5...Roughly chop the sprigs of basil and tomato flesh and add to the sauce. (If desired the bacon can be added now).
6...Bring to the boil and toss in the remaining butter to form a creamy emulsion.
7...Serve immediately in warmed soup plates. Dribble the cream over the dish and serve with toasted brioche. Serves 4.
From the menu of...

THE COUNTRY ELEPHANT
New Street, Painswick, Glos GL6 6XH.   Tel: 01425 813564
Proprietor: Mr John Rees
Chef: Mr Robert Rees
Open: Winter, Coffee 10am-12noon, Lunch 12noon-2pm, Dinner 7pm-10pm. Summer, 10am-5pm for morning coffee, lunch, afternoon tea and 7pm-10pm for dinner. Also open Christmas eve, Christmas day and NY Eve.
Booking advised but casual callers welcome if there's room. Children welcome. Credit cards accepted. Log fire in winter and outside seating in Summer. Seafood, game and vegetarian dishes.

Buried Treasure Pasta Bake

A recipe specially created by David Frost for his food loving customers.

8oz-225gm fresh short pasta e.g fusilli
1 pack 'mozzarille', marble sized mozzarella balls
1 large ball mozzarella
1oz-25gm fresh parmesan, never use pre-grated
1 spicy Italian sausage or saucisse de Toulouse, optional
1lb-450gm spicy tomato sauce for pasta, e.g Amatriciana, available
from Gastromania
1oz-25gm pan grattato,

1...Chop the sausage into medium slices and fry gently until firm.
2...Boil the pasta for about 6 minutes and drain.
3...Mix the pasta with the Amatriciana sauce and half fill a buttered souffle dish.
4...Drain the mozzarillo balls and bury in the pasta together with the sliced sausage and then cover with the rest of the pasta.
5...Cover the top with sliced mozzarella and grate the parmesan thickly over the top.
6...Bake for 18 minutes at 220c/425f/gas7
7...Sprinkle pan grattato over the top and bake for a further 2 minutes.
Serves 2-4 people and reheats well.

Variations: bury sun-dried tomatoes or pitted olives
bury meat balls or crumbled Italian sausage
bury cooked broccoli, asparagus or artichoke hearts

Pan Grattato

Keep some ciabatta for several days until stale. Chop and food process until you get coarse crumbs, discarding the finer ones by using a coarse sieve. Toast in a moderate oven until light brown. Flavour a very little olive oil by frying some crushed cloves of garlic, then discard the garlic and gently fry the crumbs in the oil so that they stay crisp.

Amatriciana Sauce

Melt 2oz-50gm finely chopped pancetta affumicata (smoked belly pork) in a
heavy pan. Turn down the heat very low and caramelise 1lb-450gm finely
chopped red onions for at least an hour. They must be mid-brown and not
burnt. Add three big cloves of finely chopped garlic, chopped red chillies to
taste and four whole large sprigs of fresh rosemary. Before the garlic has
turned brown, add ½pt-275ml red wine and 2lbs-900gm chopped Italian
tomatoes. Simmer for at least 1 hour. The long cooking is essential. Stir
occasionally to prevent sticking. Remove the rosemary before serving.
Gastromania supplies this delicious sauce ready made for you.

Recipe supplied by...

Savoury Mushroom Pyramid

This recipe is also an ideal lunch time dish.

6x 3"-7.5cm round and fried croutons
2oz-50gm peanut butter
2 tbls garlic oil
2oz-50gm butter
6x3"-7.5cm round field mushrooms
30 button mushrooms
4oz-110gm cheese herb pate

5oz-150gm soft butter
1lb-450gm cream cheese
3 cloves garlic
3 tbls chopped fresh herbs
Mix all ingredients together and chill

3oz-75gm savoury breadcrumbs:
6oz-175gm fine fresh breadcrumbs
2oz-50gm strong grated cheddar
1 pinch dry English mustard powder
1 pinch cayenne pepper

1...Fry all the mushrooms in the butter until soft.
2...Spread each crouton with the peanut butter and place a spoonful of herb pate in the middle. Place a field mushroom on top then another spoonful of the herb pate. Arrange five button mushrooms around the herb pate.
Sprinkle the savoury breadcrumbs over the top and drizzle with some garlic flavoured oil. Bake in a hot oven until bubbling.
Serve on a chopped mixed salad.

From the menu of...

BURLEIGH COURT HOTEL
Burleigh, Minchinhampton, Stroud, Glos GL5 2PF.   Tel: 01453 883804 Fax: 886870
Proprietors: Ian and Fiona Hall
Chef: Mr Christopher Perkins
Open: All year
Booking advised but casual callers welcome. Children welcome. Wheelchair access.
Log fire in Winter and Outside seating in Summer.
Vegetarian dishes and special diets catered for.

Smoked Trout Pate

Helen uses the organically fed trout from Ruskin Mills trout farm for this recipe.

8oz-225gm smoked trout
2.½oz-50gm cream cheese
1 dssrt spn of soured cream
juice of 1 small lemon
generous amount black pepper

1...Simply put all the ingredients into a food processor and turn on until the ingredients form a smooth pate. Decorate with watercress and serve with wholemeal bread.

From the menu of...

RUSKIN MILL COFFEE SHOP
Millbottom, Nailsworth, Glos GL6 0LA.   Tel: 01453 832571
A Rudolf Steiner Charitable Educational Trust
Founded by: Cotswold Chine School and Ruskin Mill
Chef: Helen Bermingham assisted by Lucy Birtles
The coffee shop is a vibrant meeting place in the heart of the Mill for the workers at the Mill as well as visitors. Excellent vegetarian food is prepared daily from organic vegetables grown by Ruskin Mill. Bread is also baked daily.

Charlotte of Cornish Crab served with Warm Potato and Green Bean Salad

2 roasted peppers
Filling:
9oz-250gm white crab meat
½ avocado, finely diced
½ granny smith. finely diced
12 rocket leaves, shredded finely
¼ iceberg, shredded finely
4oz-110gm mayonnaise
juice of ¼ lemon
1 anchovy fillet

Dressing:
1 clove garlic
3oz-75gm shallots, chopped
2fl oz-50ml white wine
1 fl oz-25ml white wine vinegar
9fl oz-200ml olive oil
1 pinch saffron

New potatoes
4fl oz-100ml soured cream
juice ½ lemon
6 cloves of garlic, finely sliced
9fl oz-200ml olive oil
7oz-200gm green beans
5oz-150gm rocket leaves
sea salt and mignonette of black pepper

1...Mix the crab meat with the avocado, apple, iceberg and rocket.
2...Blend together the anchovy and mayonnaise and lightly bind the crab.
Season and lighten the mixture with lemon juice.
3...Line 4 tall rings with the roasted halves of red pepper.
4...Push the crab meat mixture tightly into the rings
5...The dressing; Sweat the garlic and shallots in 1 fl oz-25ml olive oil.
Add the saffron. Deglaze with white wine then reduce until evaporated.
Add the white wine vinegar and the rest of the oil. Season and keep warm.
6...Garnish; sort through the rocket leaves. Lightly cook the beans and slice
on the bias. Keep cold until needed. Cook the potatoes in their jackets then
peel, slice and lay in a tray. Pour the previously prepared dressing over the
potatoes to flavour.

7...Garlic; heat olive oil in a pan then fry the garlic slices until blond and crisp. Place on absorbent paper and season.

8...Presentation; Arrange the dressed rocket leaves in the centre of the plate. Place the crab in the centre. Warm the beans and potatoes in the dressing. Arrange around the crab. Drizzle over the dressing and then the soured cream. Scatter with the garlic crisps and the sea salt.

From the kitchen of...

LE CHAMPIGNON SAUVAGE
24-26 Suffolk Road, Cheltenham, Glos GL50 2AQ.   Tel/Fax: 01242 573449
Proprietors: Mr and Mrs D Everitt-Mathias
Chef: David Everitt-Mathias
Open: All year. Lunch Mon-Fri 12.30pm-1.30pm and Dinner Mon-Sat 7.30pm-9.15pm.
Booking advised but casual callers welcome if there's room. Children welcome. Wheelchair access.
Credit cards accepted.
Serves award winning French country food. Their Warm pistachio tart with orange and liquorice sorbet won the Egon Ronay dessert of the year 1996.

Lower Severn Fishing

To many people a river is just a river, flowing aimlessly through the land, little realising how much life it sustains, as well as livelihoods. In the past it was a major rout for transporting goods. Railways and canals have reduced its commercial use, that is with the exception of commercial fishing.

One of the Severn's many claims to fame is its 'bore', one of the most impressive in Europe. This tidal wave sweeps up the river twice in every twenty four hours during the Spring tides, and is at its most spectacular during the Spring and Autumn equinoxes.

The quality of the river has been well maintained and the NRA are doing much to improve it further. Consequently almost every kind of British freshwater fish thrives in these waters.

Fishing in the lower river is largely commercial and regulations are very strict. Coarse fishing is allowed on the Upper river and a licence must be obtained. The revenues from these licenses are essential for the upkeep of the river.

Apart from the famous elver, eels are caught on their way back to sea and salmon is caught on its way up river from its spawning grounds at sea. Eels were traditionally caught by basket traps, usually made by the fishermen themselves. Today constructions made from galvanised iron wire and netting are used. Eel stocks have declined recently and in 1990 the NRA undertook a restocking programme with tiny eels that were caught in the estuary early in the year and allowed to grow before being released back at a size where they stood more chance of survival.

Each year approximately three thousand wild salmon are caught commercially and roughly one thousand are caught by rod and line on the upper Severn. Farmed salmon has in a way devalued the delight of luxury of salmon, but the flavour of wild salmon will never change. It is worth paying the little extra to get a good wild sturdy salmon than rather than a farmed flabby fleshed poor relation.

Several commercial methods are used to catch this delicious wild salmon. Fixed engines or Putchers/ Putts, as they are traditionally called, catch more than 50% of the salmon. Putchers are basketwork traps in the shape of a cone. Several hundred are mounted on a frame work to form a rank or fishing weir. They are then sighted between high and low water. As the tide ebbs the baskets are exposed and the fish caught can be removed. Putts are much larger contraptions and are positioned with the mouth upstream to fish the ebb tide. As well as salmon, eels, dabs, flounders and other small fish and shrimps are caught. Lave nets and Draft nets catch the rest of the migrating salmon. The wild salmon season is from 1st February to 15th August inclusive. Gourmets take note!

Light Lunches
and
Vegetarian Dishes

Most of the recipes in this section can be served either as a starter or a main course simply by increasing or decreasing the proportions. Because it is lunch and not a main meal of the day it is recommended that these recipes are served with a lightly dressed side salad.

Roast Vegetables Topped with Grilled Goats Cheese

Carmella recommends this as an easy dish for readers to make.

take a combination of:
sweet red and yellow peppers
courgettes
mushrooms
salad or spanish onions
tomatoes
olive oil
1 or 2 cloves garlic
sprigs of fresh sweet basil
4 ½"-1cm thick slices of goats cheese

1   Chop the vegetables into fairly large pieces and place in a large roasting tin. They should give a good covering in the dish but not piled up. The vegetables will shrink considerably during the cooking.
2...Rub just a little olive oil through the vegetables using your fingertips. Roast in a hot oven for about 10 minutes or until they are slightly charred at the edges.
3...Remove from the oven, season with coarsely ground black pepper and salt. Crush the garlic and mix into the vegetables. Return to the oven for 2-3 more minutes.
4...Spoon the roast vegetables into individual dishes. Top with a sprig of fresh basil leaves and a slice of goats cheese.
5...Flash under a hot grill (keep your eyes on it) until the cheese begins to melt.
Serve with some good bread such as ciabatta, baguette or olive bread and crisp mixed salad leaves.

NB. other cheeses such as gruyér or roqueforte can be alternatively used.

From the menu of…

TUBBY'S
At The Waterfront
Avening Rd, Nailsworth, Glos GL6 0BS   Tel: 01453 834624 and 833775 evenings
Proprietor:Carmella and Pete Fletcher
Open: All year. Monday - Saturday 9am-6pm and Sundays 10am-5pm
Casual callers and children welcome also coach parties. Wheelchair access.
Outside seating. Fresh coffee, home-made cakes and delicious lunches.
Situated next to the Waterside Garden Centre with its exotic range of plants and gifts.

Vegetarian Cookery

Vegetarianism has become an emotive subject, and a great deal of intolerance goes with it on both side of the argument. Of course there is no argument you either choose to be a vegetarian or not, and some vegetarians go further than others. This refusal to understand the vegetarian tends to blend with the few vegetarians who try to ram their beliefs down the throats of others. Their self-righteous attitude niggles, and 'those others' throw back strongly weighted questions that enter the grey areas of vegetarianism. It all causes considerable antagonism; when really we should be grateful we have the choice.

Nevertheless, there are more vegetarians in England today than ever, especially amongst the younger generation. They constitute four percent of the population and their needs are willingly recognized in cafes, restaurants and pubs all over the country. Not only that, it's not just an omelette any more, dishes have become creative and substantial, although understandably the choice is small. Some dishes have been so imaginatively conceived that even non-vegetarians will eat a vegetarian meal at lunch time.

There are advantages to vegetarian cookery. It is quick and easy, (no more waiting for the roast to cook) and it is highly suitable to microwave cookery. Vegetarian food is fresh tasting and full of roughage. The one thing it does lack is essential ascorbic acid, normally derived from meat, but it can be obtained from mushrooms.

Vegetarianism has to be approached sensibly. Vegetables, unlike meat and dairy produce have no protein which is essential for the development of the body, and if a vegetarian is involved in manual work the body needs to be strong. Protein can be obtained from nuts, but one nut to be carefully measured is coconut which has high cholesterol forming fats.

Pulses, pasta and pastry are great vehicles for vegetarian meals and the vegetables provide a colourful and tempting repast. There's also a wide variety of cheeses available for the less strict vegetarian, and many new ways of serving them other than just grated onto a bed of lettuce. In fact there is no shortage of ingredients available to ensure a healthy, interesting, tasty vegetarian diet.

Mushroom and Hazelnut Strudel with Mushroom Sauce

This very rich and yummy vegetarian recipe is definitely not, just a load of lentils!

Pastry:
8oz-225gm flour
3 tbls oil
3 tbls warm water
1 tbls wine vinegar
1 egg
(melted butter for brushing)
Filling:
2 onions
celery
1 tspn cumin
1 tspn coriander
½pt-275ml soured cream
1.½lb-700gm brown mushrooms
8oz-225gm toasted chopped breadcrumbs
4oz-110gm hazelnuts, toasted
salt and black pepper
butter for cooking

1...First make the pastry. In a large bowl put the flour, oil, warm water, wine vinegar, and egg. Mix together into a firm dough, cover with a damp cloth and leave to stand for 1 hour in a warm place.
2...For the filling. Thinly slice the onion and celery and cook gently in the butter in a heavy bottomed pan.
3...Slice the mushrooms and add to the pan with the coriander and cumin. When the vegetables are soft add the breadcrumbs to thicken the mixture. Add the hazelnuts, soured cream and salt and pepper to taste.
4...Place a clean teatowel flat on a work surface and dust it with flour. Roll out half the pastry on the teatowel until it is thin enough to see the pattern through. Brush the pastry with melted butter.
5...Cover two thirds of the pastry with half of the mushroom mixture. Lift the short side of the teatowel and use to help you roll up the strudel. Transfer to a baking sheet and brush with melted butter. Make a second strudel with the remaining ingredients.
6...Cook for 30 minutes 200c/400f/gas6. Remove from the oven and brush again with melted butter. Serve with the mushroom sauce.

Mushroom sauce

1 onion, chopped
4oz-110gm mushrooms, chopped
1 level tbls flour
1 level tbls butter
½pt-275ml vegetable stock
dash of sherry
dash of tamari
pinch thyme
salt and pepper

1...Melt the butter. Add the onion, thyme and mushrooms and cook gently until soft.
2...Stir in the flour and cook for 1 minute. Add the vegetable stock and cook until the sauce becomes the thickness of cream. Add more stock if necessary. Add the sherry and tamari and salt and pepper to taste.

From the menu of...

MILLS CAFE
8 Withey's Yard, High Street, Stroud, Glos.   Tel: 01453 752222
Proprietors: Maggie and John Mills
Chef: Gilda Naumann
Open: Monday - Saturday 8.30am-6pm and 6pm - 11pm Thursday, Friday and Saturday.
Casual callers and children welcome. Credit cards accepted. Wheelchair access.
Serve coffee and croissant in the morning, hot lunches and tea and cakes in the afternoon. Outside seating in tea garden in Summer.
All food is freshly prepared and cooked on the premises. Huge selection of home made cakes. Many of them organic. Vegetarian dishes.

Cheese and Pepper Omelette

5 eggs
salt and freshly ground black pepper
butter
2oz-50gm freshly grated parmesan cheese
4oz-110gm grated gruyèr cheese
½ green pepper, deseeded and thinly sliced

1...Beat the eggs lightly with the salt and pepper.

2...Stir in the parmesan cheese.

3...Melt some butter in an omelette pan and pour in the beaten eggs. Stir the eggs over the heat with a whisk when they are in the pan until nearly set.

4...While still moist on the top sprinkle over the gruyèr cheese and then over the cheese the thinly sliced pepper.

5...Heat the grill and put the omelette, while still in the pan, under for 2-3 minutes or until the cheese begins to bubble.

6...Fold the omelette over, slide onto a hot serving plate. Serve immediately. Enough for 2 people.

Recipe supplied by...

THE HOUSE OF CHEESE
13 Church Street, Tetbury, Glos GL8 8JG.   Tel/Fax: 01666 502865
Proprietors: Philip and Jenny Grant
Open: All year. 9am-5pm.
Specialist Cheese shop. Over 100 varieties. Including British Farmhouse and French Cheeses.

The Herb Garden

The use of herbs in cookery goes as far back as the history of food has ever been recorded. For a long time tradition told us what herbs went best with which food. For example sage and onion stuffing with pork, mint sauce with lamb, tarragon with chicken, parsley with fish. However, as is always the case, things change, rules get broken and now, in the late twentieth century the domestic kitchen has become a huge laboratory of experimentation. At the moment herb cookery has its flavours all over the place as we try swopping them around, some old, others quite new to us. Modern English cookery is mixing, for example, French cookery with Indian cookery, and Thai cookery with English cookery; it is all very exciting.

Gardeners too are paying more attention to what they grow; finding larger corners to plant their garden of herbs amongst the rows of vegetables. The old tradition of a knot garden made from fragrant herbs is beginning to form a small oasis in the modern ornamental garden.

Selsley Herb Farm in Selsley, Stroud demonstrates how easily a delightful herb garden can be created. Visitors are welcome to explore the gardens and gather ideas on their way. They have a well stocked nursery where you can purchase many unusual herbs. Their Herb shop in Nailsworth has for sale many herb inspired products.

Pesto Sauce

2 cups fresh basil
½ cup fresh parsley
½ cup olive oil
1 tbls pine nuts
1 tspn salt
½ cup grated Parmesan cheese

Puree together in a blender the first five ingredients. Then stir in the cheese. It's as simple as that! Best used fresh with pasta or as a salsa to go with fish or meat.
It will keep in the fridge for three days.

Creamy Bean Pie

This rather different pie is delicious and at the same time highly nutritious. Serve with jacket potatoes and salad. Most of the ingredients in this recipe are available at the Wholefood shop.

6oz-175gm mixed dried beans
12oz-350gm short-crust pastry
1½oz-40gm vegetable margarine
1lb-450gm onions. finely chopped
2 cloves garlic, crushed
6oz-175gm vegetarian cheddar
3 tspns freshly chopped parsley
2 fl oz-50ml natural yogurt
salt and pepper
beaten free range egg to glaze

1...Soak the bean mixture overnight in plenty of water.
2...Rinse the soaked beans thoroughly. Add fresh water to cover and bring to the boil. Boil rapidly for 10 minutes then reduce the heat and simmer for 40 minutes. Drain and leave to cool.
3...Roll out the pastry to line a 9"-22.5cm flan dish and reserve the trimmings. Blind bake the pastry case 200c/400f/gas6 for 15 minutes.
4...Meanwhile melt the margarine and sauté the onions and garlic gently until soft. Remove from the heat and beat in the cheese until melted. Add the parsley and cooked mixed beans, then add the yogurt and seasonings.
5...Place the filling in the pastry case. Roll out the pastry trimmings to make strips to form a lattice on the top. Glaze with beaten egg and bake 200c/400f/gas6 for 30-35 minutes until brown.
Serve hot or cold.

Recipe supplied by...

THE WHOLEFOOD SHOP
The Manor House, The Square, Stow-on-the-Wold, Glos GL54 1AB   Tel:01451 832194
Proprietors: John and Sylvie Rice
Open: All year 9.30am - 5.30 pm. Credit cards accepted.

Parsnip and Cheese Roast

2lb-900gm parsnips
2 onions, chopped
salt and freshly ground pepper
4 slices streaky bacon, chopped
4oz-110gm cheddar cheese
8 tbls double cream or yogurt
To finish the dish:
6 slices bacon, halved
2oz-50gm cheddar
4 tbls porridge oats or breadcrumbs

1...Wash and peel the parsnips. Cut into small pieces and cook in salted boiling water until tender.

2...Meanwhile, melt the butter in a frying pan and add the chopped streaky bacon and the chopped onion. Cook until the onion is transparent. Set aside.

3...Pre-heat the oven to 220c/425f/gas7

4...Drain the parsnips and mash. Add the onion and bacon, then the cream and cheese, salt and pepper. Turn this mixture into a buttered oven-proof dish. Smooth over the surface and arrange the bacon on the top. Sprinkle over the cheese and oats or breadcrumbs and bake on the top shelf of the oven for 20-25 minutes or until bubbly on the top.

Serve piping hot. Also a good served for high tea.

From the kitchen of...

EDGEMOOR INN
Edge, Stroud, Glos GL6 6ND.   Tel: 01452 813576
Proprietor: C and J Bayes
Chef: J Bayes and E Canham
Open: Winter 11.30am-2.30pm and 6.30pm-11pm. Summer 11am-3pm and 6pm-11pm. Open Christmas.
Casual callers welcome. Credit cards accepted.
Outside seating and outstanding views across Painswick valley.
Good home-made dishes. Vegetarian dishes.

Gloucester Sausage and Leek Slice

12oz-350gm puff pastry
1lb-450gm Gloucester sausage
1lb-450gm leeks (with plenty of green)
1 tspn dried sage
salt and plenty of black pepper
1 beaten egg for glazing

1...Trim and thoroughly wash the leeks. Cut into 1"-2.5cm long slices. Steam the leeks until tender. Cool.

2...Remove the skins from the sausages and roughly cut to the same size as the leeks. Loosely mix with the leeks.

3...Divide the puff pastry in half. Roll each half into a long strip about 18"-45.5cm long and 8"-20.5cm wide. Put one half on a baking sheet.

4...Pile the leeks and sausage mixture down the centre of the pastry. Sprinkle over the dried sage, salt and pepper. Dampen the edges with beaten egg.

5...Cut slits across the other piece of pastry down its whole length (leaving a ½"-1cm uncut boarder down each side). Lay this piece of pastry on top of the sausage mixture and seal down the edges. Glaze with beaten egg and place in a pre-heated oven 220c/425f/gas7 for 30-35 minutes.

Serve warm with salad. Makes an ideal picnic dish.

Recipe from...

THE GLOUCESTER SAUSAGE COMPANY
Unit No1, Knightsbridge Business Centre, Cheltenham, Glos GL51 9TA.   Tel: 01242 680770
Proprietor: Stuart Duberley
Open: Weekdays 7am-5pm. Saturday 8am-1pm
Supply the trade and catering outlets as well as the public.
Manufacturers of the famous Gloucester sausage.

Baked Egg and Smoked Ham en Cocotte

A simple and delicious dish using the best dairy produce.

4 size 1 eggs
8oz-225gm smoked, cooked ham, diced
2 tbls finely chopped onion, softened in butter
8 tbls double cream, (approx) must be double
4oz-110gm mature cheddar cheese, (be generous)
salt and pepper

1...Pre-heat oven to its highest setting
2...Divide the onion between four large cocotte dishes. Arrange the diced ham around the edge of the dish, leaving a hollow in the centre.
3...Break 1 egg in the centre of each hollow, then pour over the cream, about 2 tbls per cocotte.
4...Grate the cheddar and sprinkle generous amounts on top.
5...Place the cocottes on a baking tray and put in the oven for 15-20 minutes depending how well you like your eggs done.
To serve: put a folded napkin on a plate and serve immediately. Garnish with a sprig of fresh herbs.

Variations - smoked haddock, cooked leeks, sautéd mushrooms, cooked spinach, chopped tomatoes, prawns, left over bolognaise./ Stilton cheese, goats milk cheese, roqueforte cheese, emmental and gruyér cheese.

The Breakfast Pie

The Breakfast Pie was made to compliment the sandwich trade and aimed at the growing number of people using the delicatessen in the morning for 'breakfast' or for those energetic folk needing a substantial mid-morning snack.

Hot water crust pastry:
1.½lb-70gm flour
8oz-225gm lard
8fl oz-225ml boiling water
1 tspn salt
Filling:
1.½lb-700gm chopped bacon
8oz-225gm tomatoes, chopped
8oz-225gm mushrooms, chopped
6 eggs
seasoning

1...First make the pastry. Mix the flour with the salt. Melt the lard into the water. Bring to the boil and pour into the flour. Mix until the dough is smooth and silky. Put a quarter of the dough, covered with a damp cloth for the tops. Divide the remaining dough into six parts.
2...Roll each piece (not too thin) large enough to cover a 4"-10cm mould. Smooth out any folds with your fingers. Put to one side to firm up. After ½hour ease the pastry away from the mould. Support the case with a band of greaseproof paper.
3...Mix together the bacon, tomatoes and mushrooms and divide equally between the six pastry cases. Break an egg into the top of each.
4...Roll out the reserved pastry and use as tops. Crimp the sides and make a vent in the centre of each pie. Brush with egg wash and bake for 15 minutes at 220c/425f/gas7, then reduce the heat to 180c/350f.gas4 and bake until golden brown.

Recipe supplied by...

BOMFORDS DELICATESSEN
61A Cricklade Street, Cirencester, Glos GL7 1HY   Tel 01285 656900
Proprietor: Pam and Ray Davies
Bomfords is becoming famous for their pies.
Many different cutting pies are currently on sale on the deli counter. Whole for a party. Great for a buffet. They bake to order.

Scallops Coated in Brioches, Almonds and Smoked Bacon with Autumn Salad and Caper and Gherkin Vinaigrette

An elegant lunchtime dish that could also be served as an evening starter. Once tasted, the contrast of textures and flavours will be hard to forget. Scallops are best throughout September and October.

olive oil
knob of butter
1 glass white wine
12 scallops
2oz-50gm diced bacon
2oz-50gm nibbed almonds
4oz-110gm brioche crumbs
3 egg yolks
4 slices grilled bacon
4 nests of mixed salad leaves
Vinaigrette:
1 fl oz-25ml sherry
2fl oz-50ml olive oil
1 hard boiled egg, sieved
1 tbls chopped tarragon
1 tbls chopped parsley
1oz-25gm gherkins, chopped
1oz-25gm capers, chopped

1...Clean the scallops and separate them from their coral.
2...Mix together the brioche crumbs, almonds and diced smoked bacon
3...Dry the scallops on a cloth, season and roll in the egg yolk and then dip in the brioche mixture. Put to one side.
4...Arrange the salad nests on plates leaving room in the middle for the scallops.

5..Poach the corals separately in a little white wine (don't forget to taste)

6...Slice the grilled bacon in very thin strips.

7...Mix the vinaigrette ingredients together and use to dress the salad leaves.

8...Heat some olive oil and butter in a frying pan and when hot fry the scallops until golden on all sides. The scallops should be only lightly cooked inside.

8...Place the scallops in the nest with the corals and sprinkle over the bacon. Serves 4 people.

THE COUNTRY ELEPHANT
New Street, Painswick, Glos GL6 6XH.   Tel: 01425 813564
Proprietor: Mr John Rees
Chef: Mr Robert Rees
Open: Winter Coffee 10am-12noon, Lunch 12noon-2pm, Dinner 7pm-10pm. Summer 10am-5pm for morning coffee, lunch, afternoon tea and 7pm-10pm for dinner. Also open Christmas eve, Christmas day and NY Eve.
Booking advised but casual callers welcome if there's room. Children welcome. Credit cards accepted. Log fire in winter and outside seating in Summer. Seafood, game and vegetarian dishes.

Fish and Shellfish

Fish is highly nutritious and healthy as well as being low in saturated fats. When shopping always try to buy the whole fish rather than fillets or steaks. That way you can see what sort of condition it is in. Generally speaking, eyes should be bright and slightly protruding. The scales tend to come off ultra fresh fish easily. Its body should be firm, almost stiff, definitely not floppy. White fish should smell of the sea and not at all "fishy".

At home we tend to avoid serving fish both as a starter and main course, yet if you go to a seafood restaurant this is difficult to avoid. As long as the type of fish used and the sauce served have different characteristics, there's nothing wrong with serving fish twice.

Fillet of Lemon Sole with Creamed Leeks on a Red Wine Sauce

4 x 1lb-450gm lemon soles, skinned and filleted, keep the bones for stock
3 large leeks, diced into ¼"-0.5cm cubs and washed
¼pt-150ml whipping cream
½pt-275ml fish stock
3 finely chopped shallots
1 bunch chopped chives
12 thinly sliced button mushrooms
3 rashers rindless smoked bacon, finely chopped
1 bottle red wine, preferably Beaujolais
3oz-75gm unsalted butter, softened

1...Sweat the shallots and bacon in a small saucepan.
2...Fold the sole fillets into 4 suitable portions and place in a roasting tray. Cover with the shallots and bacon and then the sliced mushrooms. Pour over the fish stock cover with tin foil and put in a hot oven 230c/450f/gas8 for 10-15 minutes or until the fish is just cooked. Remove the fillets and keep warm.
3...Place the leeks and cream in a saucepan and simmer gently until the leeks are soft but not discoloured. Season.
4...Add the wine to the pan in which the fish has been cooked, place the pan over the stove and reduce quickly with 2 of the fish bones roughly chopped, until 8-10 tbls remain.
5...Pass the sauce through a strainer and without boiling whisk in the softened butter bit-by-bit - this gives the sauce a glorious shine and ensures a rich red colour.
6...To serve: Pile the diced leeks in the centre of the plate. Arrange the fillets of sole on top and surround with the red wine sauce. Garnish with sprigs of dill and accompany with spicy mashed potato.

From the kitchen of...

THE COUNTRY ELEPHANT
New Street, Painswick, Glos GL6 6XH.   Tel: 01425 813564
Proprietor: Mr John Rees
Chef: Mr Robert Rees
Open: Winter, Coffee 10am-12noon, Lunch 12noon-2pm, Dinner 7pm-10pm. Summer, 10am-5pm for morning coffee, lunch, afternoon tea and 7pm-10pm for dinner. Also open Christmas eve, Christmas day and NY Eve.
Booking advised but casual callers welcome if there's room. Children welcome. Credit cards accepted.
Log fire in winter and outside seating in Summer. Seafood, game and vegetarian dishes.

Baked Salmon with Ginger Sauce

2lb-900gm fillet of salmon
salt and pepper
4 pinches Chinese five spice powder
4 knobs butter
4 sprigs of fresh fennel, dill or chervil
Sauce
¼pt-150ml strong fish stock
¼pt-150ml orange juice
¼pt-150ml white wine
2 tbls white wine vinegar
1" piece of fresh ginger peeled and finely grated
2 tbls honey
1 tspn cornflour
4oz-110gm butter

1…First prepare the sauce. Place in a large heavy bottomed saucepan the
fish stock, orange juice, white wine, wine vinegar, ginger and honey. Bring
to the boil reduce the heat then simmer rapidly until reduce by half. Put to
one side.

2…Remove the skin from the salmon fillet and cut into four portions.
Grease a baking tray and lay on the salmon fillets. Smear a knob of butter
on top of each fillet and lay on top the sprigs of chosen herb then sprinkle
with the salt, pepper and Chinese five spice powder. Put in a pre-heated
oven 220c/425f/gas7 and bake for 10 minutes.

3…Meanwhile re-heat the sauce. Mix the cornflour with a drop of water
and add to the sauce. Simmer until the sauce thickens slightly. Then add the
butter. Bring to a rapid boil.

4…Arrange the salmon fillets on warm plates and pour over some of the
sauce. Serve with new potatoes, French beans and braised fennel.

King Prawn, John Dory, and King Scallop Seared in Olive Oil with a Light Basil Sauce and Ink Risotto Rice

A modern inspired dish with a Mediterranean influence made with superb fresh fish.

4 king prawns, shelled
4 diver caught scallops (king)
4 baby fillets of John Dory
salt and pepper
fish stock
extra virgin olive oil
black ink from squid
6oz-175gm arborio rice
4 basil leaves
unsalted butter
shallots and garlic to taste
12 spring onions
vegetable stock and lemon juice

1...First prepare the rice. Use a thick bottomed saucepan, add a little unsalted butter and pan fry some chopped shallots and garlic until soft. Add the arborio rice and a little fish stock to cover then simmer.
2...Add squid ink and stir, this will make the rice go black. Keep on adding the stock as and when it absorbs into the rice. When the rice is tender cool for about 10 minutes. Season to taste.
3...In a non stick pan add a little olive oil. When hot put in the king prawns, John Dory and scallops. Add salt and pepper and cook until golden brown. Take out and keep warm.
4...Add a ladle full of fish stock to the fish pan and reduce. Add a couple of knobs of butter and the lemon juice. Whisk until bound together. Add the chopped basil, season and serve.
5...Add the spring onions to the vegetable stock. Simmer for a few minutes. The onions should remain crunchy.

6...Arrange the ink risotto in the centre of each soup plate. Place the three fish in a triangle around the risotto, add the sauce. Garnish with the lightly cooked spring onion with a twist and serve.

From the kitchen of...

Gloucestershire Pike and Potato Cakes with Tomato and Basil Hollandaise

1lb-450gm pike fillet
1lb-450gm potatoes, boiled
1oz-25gm butter
4oz-110gm flour
4oz-110gm double Gloucester cheese, grated
2 eggs
Hollandaise:
8oz-225gm butter
2fl oz-50ml white wine
2fl oz-50ml white wine vinegar
pinch cracked pepper
4 egg yolks
1oz-25gm tomato puree
4 large basil leaves

1...Steam the pike and flake the flesh. Mash the potatoes while still hot with the butter. Add the flour and cheese and mix together. Add the flaked pike to this mixture. Beat the eggs and add to the mixture. Season.
2...Roll the mixture into balls and slightly flatten.
3...Lightly fry the cakes in hot oil on both sides until golden brown.
4...Meanwhile make the sauce: Put the vinegar, white wine and pepper in a saucepan and reduce by a third. Add the yolks to this reduction and whisk over a very gentle heat until the yolks become thick and foamy. You might prefer to do this in a double saucepan.
5...Melt the butter and slowly whisk it, a bit at a time into the yolks. Must be done over a very low heat.
6...Season with a few drops of lemon juice, the tomato puree and the chopped basil leaves.
7... Serve the Pike and potato cakes straight from the pan with the warm hollandaise.
From the kitchen of...

THE CLOSE HOTEL
and Restaurant
Long Street, Tetbury, Glos GL8 8AQ.   Tel:01666 502272
Proprietors: Passport Hotels ltd
Managed by: Virgin Hotels ltd
Chef: Paul Welch and team
Open: All year
Uses fresh local ingredients that promotes regional dishes and produce.

A Hygienic Kitchen

Healthy eating starts before you do the shopping and doesn't have an awful lot to do with the kind of food you eat!

Anyone involved in the catering industry is already acutely aware of the importance of strict hygiene. Not only because of the threat of closure if the Health Inspector isn't satisfied with standards, but because they have no desire to make their paying customers ill.

A health inspector would probably reel back in horror if invited to inspect a domestic kitchen as would its owner if they knew just how stiff the regulations were.

Out would go the cat, the dog, their baskets, their bowls of food and water and their owners coats, shoes and handbags. The beautifully carved chopping board would have to be burned, and all those little bits of sauce, too good to waste and shoved to the back of the fridge would definitely be out the door. Smoking would have to be banned and so would anyone with a cough or cold. In fact anything remotely considered a carrier of germs no matter how small would have to go. Even the wedding ring and not just for the washing up!

If an inspector looked into the average domestic fridge he might just die of fright! Uncovered food, raw meat next to cooked meat, temperature not cold enough, ice box 'iced-up'. Indeed the fridge will probably be in the wrong place anyway. Next to the cooker, washing machine or in direct sunlight. All of which will help to lower the temperature.

Then there's the cleaning. Mopping the floor and wiping the work-surfaces every day is not enough. Anywhere that dust and grease can congregate to provide luxury accommodation for crawling insects - that get into mischief in the night - must be kept spotlessly clean. For the caterer this means pulling out fridges, freezers, washing machines and cookers and thoroughly cleaning behind them at least once a week. Walls, windows, door frames and light fittings must all be clean, and if you've got a dirty oven, the worst job of all, you'll get a sever rap on the knuckles.

Such extremes of cleanliness in a domestic kitchen which more often t resembles Piccadilly station, is almost possible to adhere to. However, a few simple and sensible rules are worth considering.

PETS: It's impossible to keep pets out of the kitchen. The smell of food is too compelling, it's probably their favourite room in the house. Train your dog at an early age not to jump up to sniff counters and cats not to walk over them. This may be more difficult if bad habits have already developed. If this is the case be a little more rigorous with your cleaning. Just before commencing work wipe the surface with disinfectant. (Clear dettol is ideal).

DISH CLOTHS, TEATOWELS AND WASTE BINS: All wonderful sanctuaries for germs. If you have used a dish cloth to wipe up blood from raw meat, wash it thoroughly before using it again or use kitchen roll. Use a clean teatowel every day and don't be tempted to dry your hands on it. Ideally wash dishes in water that is too hot to put your bare hands in (protect them with rubber gloves) then let the plates drip dry. Waste bins should be covered at all times to deter flies, a species that has an acute sense of smell.

FRIDGES: Store raw meat, i.e. sausages, bacon, gammon steaks, joints of meat, chicken and barbecue meat in spices in a plastic container kept specially for this job.

You might be surprised to know that the warmest part of the fridge is next to the ice box (warm air rises, remember!?). You could buy a cheap thermometer from the supermarket and keep it on the top shelf and use as a guide. Never put warm or hot food straight into the fridge as this raises the temperature and reduces effectiveness. Also don't leave the fridge door open when, for instance getting the milk out, it only takes a second for the cold air to rush out and hot air in.

FREEZERS: Freezing does not kill bacteria's. Bacteria's only remains dormant when frozen and indeed some bacteria's, such as listeria can still grow, albeit slowly. Don't freeze food for too long as it can deteriorate, although this might not necessarily be harmful. Keep a track of when you put food in the freezer and always cover food to be frozen otherwise it could suffer from freezer burn which can destroy the texture of food.

HYGIENE: Always wash your hands after handling raw meat.

Naturally you must always wash your hands after using the toilet. It is essential that young children, who love to suck their fingers, learn this habit. It is very easy to pass nasty germs onto plates touched by contaminated hands.

VERMIN: If you live in the country you can be troubled with infestations of mice and rats, and in the town cockroaches as well as rats. Then there is the continuous troop of flies, flour beetles and silver fish. Ideally keep food off the ground in high cupboards. Keep everything well sealed and don't leave food lying around as a tempting midnight feast. Even a crumb of bread on the floor will be an attraction. And believe me it doesn't take long for the word to get around. Ants are particularly good at communications.

If you have a serious problem contact the public health who have a department that can deal quite efficiently with these unwanted guests.

SHOPPING: Be wary and keep your eyes open. Do the staff look scruffy, dangling hair, bare hands at meat counters. Blowing their nose. Dirty floors and counters and dirty toilets in pubs and restaurants should all make you suspicious of their standards of hygiene.

FRESH FRUIT: Is often hand picked and not always washed afterwards. Strawberries may for instance may have been picked by contaminated hands, yours or someone else's. Therefore wash all fruits and salads before consuming.

PARANOIA: It is right that people in the catering trade should be paranoid about hygiene, their livelihood is at stake.

But we should be more relaxed. All my life I have eaten raw eggs, rare meat, well hung game, under-cooked pork and even food that has been in and out of the freezer a couple of times and have never had food poisoning as a result.

Some people are of the school of thought that too much hygiene is bad for us. 'Death by Hygiene' may not seem such a funny idea if the body is not allowed to build up a certain resistance to some common bacteria's and germs, and too much hygiene will make sure of that.

Fresh Water Eels in Tomato Sauce

1lb.8oz-700gm fresh water eel. Skinned and cut into 2"-5cm
thick pieces
seasoned flour
oil for cooking
2 tins chopped Italian tomatoes or 1 tin a 8oz-225gm fresh
chopped tomato (skins removed)
1 tbls tomato puree
1 medium onion finely chopped
1 or 2 cloves garlic crushed
1 tbls dried herbs i.e. thyme, basil, tarragon or dill.
¼pt-150ml dry white wine
1 tbls capers
salt and pepper

1...First make the sauce. Soften the onion in a little oil. Add the crushed
garlic and cook for 3 more minutes. Add the chopped tomatoes, tomato
puree, dried herbs, white wine and capers. Simmer for about 20 minutes or
until the sauce reduces and thickens slightly.
2...Meanwhile toss the eel pieces in the seasoned flour. Heat some oil in a
frying pan and when hot quickly cook the fish until golden all over.
3...Pour the sauce into the frying pan and simmer until the fish is cooked.
About 15 minutes (eel takes a little longer to cook than most fish)
Serve with buttery ribbon noodles and green beans or calabrese.
Serves 4.

Elvers

In 1977 during the Easter Monday Elver-eating contest twenty Two year old Keith Lane beat the world record by downing a pound of elvers in 31 seconds. This annual elver-eating contest reflects just how traditional and important this delicacy is to the region. In fact it is the only 'fry' apart from whitebait that is legally allowed to be caught as food.

As small as it looks the elver is actually three years old when it returns to the river Severn to finish growing to adult hood. The first year of arrival they

To maintain the elver and therefore the eel population fishing for elvers is restricted to a short Spring season from March to April. Nevertheless during this time many tons(currently 10-20) of them are caught.

Elvers tend to do most of their movement at night when the waters are warm and this is when they are fished, usually on Spring tides. Occasionally they are fished during the day tides, most successfully when the tide is on the ebb. Elvers swim against the tide so the fishers simple net is dipped into the river with the mouth downstream until about three-quarters submerged. The full net is then lifted and emptied into a bucket. (This is the traditional method. Today trays are used for easy transport).

Between Sharpness and Tewkesbury there are several commercial elver and eel fisheries. There are two kinds; the silver eel fisheries in the tidal waters of the Severn and Trent and the yellow eel fisheries in still waters and the canals. Eel and elver stocks have dropped slightly over the years and research by the National River Authority has shown it has a lot to do with the weirs which impedes the elvers swim up river. They are now constructing passes in the weirs for the elvers and restocking young fish as part of an on-going programme.

Elvers are transparent and when cooked turn a milky white. They can be tossed in seasoned flour in a similar manner to whitebait and deep fried, served with brown bread and butter and a wedge of lemon. A more traditional method which is rich and nutritious, is to lightly cook them in bacon fat until they change colour, then beaten eggs are added to make a kind of omelette. They can also be made into a pie or a form of paté (or cheese as it was called in those days) by cooking slowly with herbs and spices then packed into pots.

Meat, Poultry and Game

A menu is often designed around the meat or main course so this is probably the easiest dish to decide upon. It is best to make your choice depending upon seasonal availability. For example, game in the Autumn, poultry and pork at Christmas, lamb in Spring and early Summer, and beef, once the most popular of meats but less so now that red meat has lost favour with the healthies, is available all year round.

Meat is less fatty these days, which is a great shame since most of the flavour is carried in the fat. It is much better to eat and enjoy a good flavoursome, fatty, roast, but less often than you would a fatless, tasteless roast.

These days meat is sold ultra fresh, which invariably means it hasn't been hung unless it has been through the hands of a good traditional family butcher. Meat is hung to improve the flavour and tenderness.

Sage and Onion Pork Chop

A simple yet tasty dish.

4 loin pork chops
beaten egg
sage and onion stuffing:
4oz-110gm stale breadcrumbs
1 onion finely chopped
salt and black pepper
1 tbls dried sage leaves
1 stock cube finely crumbled
Alternatively use a packet of sage and onion stuffing

1...Mix the stuffing ingredients together.
2...Dip the pork chops in beaten egg and then into the stuffing mix so that the chops are liberally coated.
3...Place on a greased baking tray and bake in a pre-heated oven at 190c/375f/gas5 for 45-50 minutes or until golden brown.
Serve with new potatoes and beans or side salad.

From the kitchen of...

THE COFFEE BEAN
High Street, Minchinhampton, Stroud, Glos GL6 9BN.   Tel: 01453 883382
Proprietor/Cook: Joy Picken
Open: All year Tuesday - Friday 10am-5pm and Saturday 10am-12.30pm
Serving homemade cakes, biscuits and general goodies, plus a meal of the day which is best ordered in advance. Look out for their ever popular "Goo" now a trade mark of the Bean.
A warm welcome, a friendly smile and good home-style cooking are waiting for all their customers.

The Value of Meat

More than anything it is important to eat a balanced diet, yet because of the bad, sometimes uninformed publicity over recent years more people have ceased to eat meat - therefore, unbalancing their diet.

Meat is extremely good for you and meat products in general, such as milk and eggs are essential for a healthy diet. If you cut them out as vegans do then artificial substitutes have to be taken to replace lost nutriments.

Looking at it scientifically the body needs the building blocks of protein which are amino acids. The body is unable to manufacture these acids so it has to get them from 'high-quality' protein which is found in meat. Protein is essential to everyone but particularly to children who have fast growing bodies. The body also needs vitamin B12 and meat products are virtually the only dietary source: plant foods lack vitamin B12.

Minerals are also important. Iron, it is true is available in grains, nuts and pulses (via baked products) but by far the best source is meat, simply because it is chemically bound to the blood-protein haemoglobin and is therefore, rapidly absorbed into the blood. This is not the case with iron found in plants and lack of iron can cause anaemia.

The amount of meat required for a healthy diet depends on whether you are male or female, a pregnant woman or a growing child, the last two. by the way need the most. The average person within these categories requires 6-9 oz of meat (or fish) per day. We are not talking 16oz T Bone steaks here but a few slices of roast beef or an average sized chicken breast.

Unbeknown to many people, most meat is reared in happy conditions. Fields full of cows (beef) and sheep (lamb) is proof of that, and in fact have always been reared that way; and these days it is not uncommon to see pigs rooting around in the open fields. Battery chicken do still exist and are very cheap, but for a little extra money you can easily purchase a free range chicken. The more of you that do, the more common and eventually cheaper free range chickens (and eggs) will become.

It is not in the farmer's interest not to look after his animals unless he wants to fork out money for hefty vets bills, and an animal that has been stressed in the slaughter house, as so many people claim, results in inedible meat, what's the point of that!

In the same way that a damaged apple is inedible so is damaged meat and great care is taken that this should not happen. At least the meat you eat has not been sprayed with insecticide and if an animal is ill the antibiotics it is given to help its recovery are no more harmful than the ones the doctor gives us to aid our own recovery.

Meat is essential for the development of strong healthy children and very important to people in active work, be it for pleasure or pay.

Five Valley Pork

2lb-900gm fillet of pork (tenderloin)
generous knob of butter
4fl oz-100ml calvados
12fl oz-325ml double cream
12oz-350gm mature farmhouse cheddar

1...Cut the pork fillet into bite sized strips.
2...Heat the butter in a large heavy bottomed pan. Add the pork and saute until cooked through. You might have to do this in 2 or 3 batches. Keep each batch warm.
3...Put all the cooked pork into the pan, add the calvados, heat through and flambé.
4...Pour over the double cream.
5...Season to taste (careful with the salt as the cheese you are about to add will increase the saltiness). Pour the pork mixture into a serving dish.
6...Grate the cheddar cheese and sprinkle liberally over the pork. Place under a hot grill until golden and bubbling.
Serve immediately with broccoli and rice or small pasta. Serves 4 hungry people.

From the menu of...

THE COOKERY NOOK
3 Cossack Square, Nailsworth, Glos GL6 0DB.   Tel: 01453 832615
Proprietors: Richard and Joanne Martin
Chefs: Richard Martin
Open: All year. Lunch 12 noon-2.30pm and Dinner 7pm-Midnight
Casual callers and children. Credit cards accepted and wheelchair access.
Licensed with separate bar area. Seafood, game and vegetarian dishes. All home prepared and cooked food.

The Orchard Pig

Unfortunately not lean enough for todays modern tastes the Gloucester Old Spot became a dying breed and is now classes as a rare breed by the Rare Breeds Society. Because of its Autumn diet on windfall apples it became romantically known as the orchard pig.

Orchards, in particular, apple orchards thrive in the rich and heavy soils of the Severn valley and most orchard owners would keep a Gloucester Old Spot to tidy up after the apple picking.

It is said that its flesh had a slight apple flavour because of such a diet. Whether it did or not apple sauce has for a long, long time been a perfect accompaniment to roast pork.

Gloucester Old Spot is a sprightly looking pig, quite slender considering it has a higher fat content than modern pigs. It has a long jaw and irregular black spots scattered on its pink rump. A famous regional dish called bath chaps (pigs cheeks) originated from the Gloucester Old Spot because of its long jaw. They can still be bought in traditional butchers either smoked or unsmoked and cooked or uncooked.

Simple Apple sauce

2 large cooking apples, peeled and sliced; 1 or 2 tbls castor sugar squeeze of lemon juice; pinch of salt, knob of butter

Place all the ingredients in an saucepan and place over a low heat. Cover with a lid to keep the moisture in and cook until the apples have collapsed. Beat with a wooden spoon until smooth. Cool and serve with delicious roast pork and crisp crackling. (The ingredients can be put in a dish, covered and cooked in the microwave)

Special Apple Sauce

2 large cooking apples, peeled and sliced: 1 large onion finely chopped: good sprig of fresh sage, finely shredded; 1-2 tbls castor sugar squeeze of lemon juice, 1oz-25gm butter: pinch salt.

Soften the onion in the butter. Add the rest of the ingredients and simmer gently in a covered saucepan until the apples are soft and pulpy. Beat with a

Roasted Tenderloin of Old Spot Pork with Woodland Mushrooms and Tomato

2 Gloucester Old Spot Pork Tenderloins
14oz-400gm leaf spinach
8oz-225gm pigs caul
1 sprig of fresh sage, chopped
1 egg
1 onion, finely chopped
6oz-175gm assorted woodland mushrooms
4 tomatoes
½pt-275ml beef stock
¼pt red wine
salt and pepper
1oz-25gm butter

1...Trim all sinew and fat off the pork tenderloins and cut 4 lengths of fillet approximately 3-4"/7-10cm long. Save the remaining meat.

2...Puree the remaining meat with the egg in a blender until smooth. Add the seasoning and chopped sage

3...Stretch out the pigs caul to approximately 4x6"/10x15cm squares.

4...Line the caul with cooked spinach leaves and then spread the pork and sage mousse onto the spinach.

5...Place a trimmed portion of the pork fillet on top of the square of mousse, slightly towards the top. Fold in the edges of the square and roll up to enclose all of the fillet into a neat parcel. Repeat with the remaining three fillets.

6...Melt the butter in a frying pan and seal the pork parcels, season well.

7...Place them on a baking tray and put in the oven pre-heated to 200c/400f/gas6 for 12-15 minutes.

8...Put the chopped onions in a small saucepan with the red wine. Boil until the wine has virtually evaporated. Add the stock and reduce the mix by half.

9...Wash and roughly chop the mushrooms and add to the sauce. Simmer until the mushrooms are tender, about 4 minutes. Season to taste.

10...Remove the skin and seeds from the tomatoes and finely dice the flesh - save for garnish.
11...When the pork is done, remove from the oven and slice each fillet into 6 x½"-1cm slices. Arrange on hot plates.
12...Spoon the mushrooms and sauce around the meat and sprinkle over the chopped tomato.

From the kitchen of...

THE CLOSE HOTEL
and Restaurant
Long Street, Tetbury, Glos GL8 8AQ.   Tel:01666 502272
Proprietors: Passport Hotels ltd
Managed by: Virgin Hotels ltd
Chef: Paul Welch and team
Open: All year
Uses fresh local ingredients that promotes regional dishes and produce.

All Year Lamb

Modern breeding methods have put lamb on the table all year round. Yet the very best is still only available for half the year, from April to September.

New seasons lamb starts off at an extravagant price and is a real treat at Easter. By July and August the price has bottomed out. Young Spring lamb is the most succulent and tender of meats. It needs little cooking and just melts in the mouth - a small leg will barbecue beautifully in less than and hour. The 'prime' cuts come from the saddle and that too requires the barest of flames to surrender the delicate flesh to the bluntest of knives.

When shopping choose the palest pink cuts veiled with a thin, creamy gossamer coating of fat.

There's some disagreement over the various stages in the ageing of lamb. My own rule of thumb is that young Spring lamb will be no more than 15-20 weeks old and just weaned off its mothers milk. After that and up to 8 months old it will have pent its days grazing on continuously sprouting fresh green grass, I class this as straight forward lamb. After it is twelve months old I treat lamb from a cooking point of view as mutton (although strictly speaking mutton can be 3-4 years old and has a deep, rich flavour). Some people, New Zealanders for instance, who import a great deal of lamb to this country, will classify this 'young mutton' as hogget.

The three most elegant cuts of lamb come from the saddle, the best end neck and the gigot (leg). Perfect for an elegant dinner party. The gigot if cut into thick steaks is wonderful if briefly cooked on a open charcoal grill. The more homely cuts such as the shoulder, the whole leg and chump chops have more fat and to my mind the most flavour.

As the lamb gets older, short, fierce bursts of heat, ideal for Spring lamb are less viable and longer slower cooking of this mature lamb is more viable. I recommend that you cook lamb Greek style - long and slow, so that the delicious fat seeps through the joint, rendering the meat meltingly tender and full of its own natural juicy flavours.

Of all our farmed animals sheep are just about the nearest we will ever get to an organic beast without actually going to a certified organic breeder. They are sturdy little creatures, fare for themselves on open fields and craggy hills on a staple diet of naturally growing grass and wild herbs.

Many ingredients have a natural affinity with lamb. Some such as mint in mint sauce and onions in onion sauce are an English tradition. Or tomatoes and Aubergines for a Mediterranean flavour. The Welsh serve it with laverbread and oranges and the French with tarragon and asparagus. In India they prefer to eat mutton enhanced with pungent spices. My own preference is for a 12 month old shoulder, spit roasted, very slowly in the open air with copious amounts of rosemary and garlic.

Spring Lamb with Lemon, Mint and Soured Cream Sauce

An elegant dish worth saving for up for your best Spring Dinner Party

1 saddle of the first of the Springs lamb, chined and all bones removed
2 good tbls freshly chopped mint, chopped at the last minute
¼pt-275ml chicken stock
5fl oz pot soured cream
1 level tbls flour
2oz-50gm butter
1 sugar cube
1 large lemon, the finely grated zest and the juice
salt and <u>white</u> pepper

1...Trim off any excess fat from the lamb (in fact there shouldn't be any on Spring lamb and what small amount of fat there is needed for flavour). Season and bring up to room temperature if it has been taken from the fridge.

2...Pre-heat the oven to 200c/400f/gas6. Place the saddle in a roasting tin, skin side facing up and roast for 20-30 minutes depending on how well done you like it. Pink is best for a succulent finish. Take out and rest for 10 minutes.

3...Meanwhile make the sauce. This can in fact be made well in advance. Melt the butter in a saucepan then add the flour. Cook gently for 2 or 3 minutes without browning the flour. Add the stock and lemon juice whisking all the time to amalgamate to a smooth sauce. Add the lemon rind, lower the heat and simmer for 20 minutes.

4...Stir in the sugar cube, mint and soured cream. heat for a further 5 minutes to extract the flavour from the mint. Adjust the seasoning.

5...Carve the meat into 1"-2.5cm thick slices and arrange in a circle in the centre of a hot plate. Tip any escapes juices into the sauce and pour around the lamb. Garnish with a mint leaf and a wafer thin slice of lemon. Serve with new potatoes and minted peas.

Lamb, Kumquat and Barley Casserole

Mutton if you can get it is ideal for this warming Winter dish

1 leg of mutton or lamb, a leg of mutton will feed more people
1 large onion, finely chopped
1 or 2 cloves garlic, crushed in salt
½pt-275ml chicken stock
¼pt-150ml orange juice
½pt-150ml white wine
8oz-225gm kumquats
4oz-110gm closed cap mushrooms
2oz-50gm pearl barley
½tspn dried thyme, more if using fresh
1 level tbls molasses sugar
oil

1...Remove the meat from the bone and cut into large dice. Heat the oil in a frying pan and brown the meat, a few pieces at a time. Put the browned meat to one side.

2...Add a drop more oil to the pan if necessary and soften the onions, allowing them to become golden brown. Add the mushrooms and cooks for a few more minutes until the mushrooms have wilted.

3...Put this onion and mushroom mixture in the bottom of a casserole with the pearl barley. Lay the lamb on top and sprinkle with the thyme and sugar. Scatter the whole kumquats over the top and then pour over the stock, orange juice and wine.

4...Seal the casserole tightly with tin foil then the lid on top (to prevent the steam escaping and the casserole drying up). Put in a pre-heated oven 180c/350f/gas4 for about 1 hour 30mins. Test for tenderness at this stage. Be careful not to overcook or the all the flavour of the lamb will be lost into the sauce.

Serve with broccoli and carrots.

A Fleece of Gold

In the middle ages there were so many sheep in the Cotswolds you could barely see the grass and they certainly outnumbered the human population. They were not however kept for food but for their glorious 'golden fleece'. Golden not because of their colour, albeit rather attractive, but because of the bountiful revenue that it brought into the country. The Cotswold sheep was named after the Cotswold Hills and was an ancient breed, a descendant from the Roman longwool sheep. It was exported to Europe, as far back as Norman times and won the reputation as the best quality wool in Europe. The reputation did good for the Cotswolds region for several hundred years. It was such a success that its tax revenue accounted for fifty percent of the country's total tax collection.

It is easy to understand why the fleece of the Cotswold was so popular. It was heavier than any other with a good curl, a thick lion's mane and a healthy lustrous glow. The Cotswold was in fact, to become the largest sheep in England.

Thanks to the success of this export industry to Europe the Cotswolds region and other parts of Gloucestershire were developed. Wool merchants had churches rebuilt in fine style. And later as the wool trade collapsed due to the raised government taxes and the cloth-making industry took over, wealthy cloth merchants built themselves fine houses of Cotswold stone. The valleys of the Cotswolds were ideal sites for the water mills that were needed to operate the weaving machines. The industry thrived for many years and didn't begin to decline until the later end of the industrial revolution when synthetic fibres were made and cheap cotton imports flooded the market.

Today the Cotswold, that once freckled the hills, is a protected rare breed. A top quality cloth is still spun in the Stroud valley and this process of, carding, spinning and weaving can still be seen at Filkins.

Wild Duck with Nuts and Port

This is one of Waterman's most popular Autumn dishes. which celebrates Gloucestershire's seasonal bounty.

2 wild ducks, mallards
1 each carrot, onion, celery stick, finely chopped
generous sprigs of rosemary and thyme
1lb-450gm celeriac, peeled and chopped
½ lemon
freshly grated nutmeg
¼pt-150ml double or whipping cream   )   can be omitted
2oz-50gm butter or marg   )   but not as much fun
handful toasted hazelnuts, half of them roughly ground
2 glasses port

1...Cut off the duck breasts and legs, or ask your tame butcher to do so.
2   Put the carcasses, the legs, chopped carrot, onion and celery and the herbs into a saucepan, cover with good stock, water + stock cube, bring to the boil and then simmer for 1 hour or until the legs are tender. This can be done a day ahead for added flavour.
3...Cook the celeriac in lightly salted water with the lemon (to stop discolouring) until soft. Puree the celeriac while still hot in a food processor then add the cream and butter, ground hazelnuts, grated nutmeg and seasoning to taste. Whiz until the texture is silky like wallpaper paste! You may like to add extra lemon juice to balance the creaminess and enhance the flavour.
4...Season the duck breasts. Brush with a little oil and place under a medium grill for about 5 minutes each side. Rest for 5-10 minutes. Mallard cooked rare or medium is quite delicious and more tender.
5...Meanwhile, remove the legs from the saucepan, strain the liquid into a clean pan and reduce to about ¼pt-150ml. Skim off any fat. Add one glass of port and drink the other while carefully stirring in the cream. Adjust seasoning.

6...To serve: Put a tablespoonful of celeriac puree on each warmed plate and if you're feeling brave, thinly slice the breasts (otherwise leave whole) and fan out around the puree. Pop a leg on top, bone sticking up artistically. Spoon some sauce around the breast, scatter whole hazelnuts around the edge and poke a tiny sprig of herb into the puree. Serve with herb roasted potatoes, spiced red cabbage and broccoli, and enjoy a gutsy Rhone red, a South African Pinotage or an Australian Shiraze. Cheers! Serves 4.

From the kitchen of...

WATERMAN'S RESTAURANT
Old Market, Nailsworth, Glos GL6 0BX.   Tel: 01453 832808
Proprietors: John and Sarah Waterman
Chef: Sarah Waterman
Open: All year. Tuesday - Saturday from 7.30pm and for Christmas day lunch.
Booking advised but casual callers welcome. Children welcome. Credit cards accepted. Wheelchair access.
Game in season and vegetarian dishes. Scrumptious puds. Theme dinners. Well stocked wine cellar.
A delightful 16th century Cotswold stone cottage with walled garden and stream. Outside seating in the Summer.

Spiced Wood Pigeon with Beetroot Barley Risotto, Garlic Confit and Bitter Chocolate Jus

A good example of how complex David's dishes can be.

4 Wood pigeons (supremed)
9fl oz-500ml pigeon stock, made from the carcase and legs
1fl oz-30ml port
1fl oz-30ml sherry vinegar
8fl oz-225ml red wine
heart and liver of 4 pigeons
½oz-15gm bitter chocolate
½oz-15gm unsalted butter
spice mix: ½oz-10gm each of ground cumin, coriander, cinnamon and cardamom
barley risotto:
5oz-150gm pearl barley
3oz-75gm onion
5oz-150gm diced beetroot
½pt-300mls chicken stock
2oz-50gm butter
garnish:12 cloves garlic, 4oz-110gm cooked and diced beetroot, 5oz-150gm goose fat

1...First make the sauce. Fry the bones from the pigeons until golden then deglaze with the vinegar. Reduce until evaporated. Deglaze with the port and reduce until evaporated. Add the wine and reduce by half. Add the pigeon stock and simmer until the correct consistency. Add the chocolate and then the butter. Pass the sauce through a sieve, then taste and adjust seasoning. Lighten with a little more vinegar if needed.
2...Saute the livers and hearts until pink.
3...Heat 4oz-110gm of goose fat in a small saucepan. Peel the garlic cloves and add to the fat. Simmer gently until the garlic is tender. Cool. Crisp up in a little of the goose fat when ready to serve.
4...Next make the risotto. Dice the beetroot and sweat with the onion. Add the barley and cook for 3-4 minutes. Add the chicken stock and cook the barley until al dente. Finish with the butter and parmesan cheese. Check the seasoning and keep warm.

5...Mix together the spice ingredients and use to season the breasts. Saute the pigeon breasts 2 or 3 minutes each side until medium rare in 1oz-20gm goose fat.

To serve: Warm the beetroot dice in the sauce. Place a little beetroot risotto on the plates. Dress the pigeon on top. Scatter over the garlic confit. Arrange the liver and heart on the plate and finally pour around the pigeon jus and the beetroot dice.

From the menu of...

LE CHAMPIGNON SAUVAGE
24-26 Suffolk Road, Cheltenham, Glos GL50 2AQ.   Tel/Fax: 01242 573449
Proprietors: Mr and Mrs D Everitt-Mathias
Chef: David Everitt-Mathias
Open: All year. Lunch Mon-Fri 12.30pm-1.30pm and Dinner Mon-Sat 7.30pm-9.15pm.
Booking advised but casual callers welcome if there's room. Children welcome. Wheelchair access. Credit cards accepted.
Serves award winning French country food. Their Warm pistachio tart with orange and liquorice sorbet won the Egon Ronay dessert of the year 1996.

Possin au Diablo

2 baby chicken
1 tbls paprika
10 fl oz-250ml dry white wine
2 cloves garlic, crushed
1 tbls oregano
1lb-500gm blended tomatoes
salt and pepper

1...Clean the baby chickens, rub with salt and place in a small roasting tin. Put in a pre-heated oven 230c/450f/gas8 for 30 minutes.
2...When the chickens have cooked drain off the excess fat. Remove the breasts from the chicken and put to one side. Keep them warm. Turn the remaining chicken upside down in the tray. Add the white wine, blended tomatoes, oregano, paprika and garlic, and place the tray back in the oven for a further 15 minutes.
3...To serve: Put the chickens on hot plates and reposition the breasts on the carcase. Pour over the sauce. Serve with a crisp side salad.
Serves 2.

From the menu of...

THE MAD HATTER WINE BAR
30 Castle Street, Cirencester, Glos GL7 1QH.   Tel: 01285 642371
Proprietors: Mr B Sylvestri and Mr B Recina
Open: All year. Noon - 11.30pm.
Children welcome. Wheelchair access. Booking advised but casual callers welcome for dinning. Credit cards accepted.
Outside seating in the Summer and Log fire in the Winter.
A variety of English and Italian dishes. Also vegetarian.

A Salad of Home Smoked Grenadine Chicken with a Black Olive Dressing

2 chicken breasts
4 fl oz-100ml grenadine
9 shallots, finely chopped
20 fl oz dry white wine
2 fl oz olive oil
15 fl oz vegetable oil
1 egg yolk
1 tbls fresh root ginger chopped
4oz-110gm pitted black olives
1 fl oz white wine vinegar
3 tspns white sugar
1 tbls dijon mustard
salad for garnish

1...Roughly chop six of the shallots and mix with the grenadine. Add half the dry white wine, the olive oil a pinch of salt and a pinch of sugar. Pour this marinade into a dish that will take the chicken breasts. Marinate the chicken for 24 hours. Keep covered.

2...Cover the bottom of a frying pan with oak sawdust. Place a wire mesh over the pan. Place the marinated chicken on the mesh and cover with foil.

3...Put the pan on a high flame. When the sawdust begins to smoke reduce the heat to a small flame and leave for approx 15 minutes.

4...Put the remaining three shallots in a food processor along with the root ginger, egg yolk, black olives, white wine vinegar, sugar and white wine. Blend until smooth. Very slowly mix in the vegetable oil to make an emulsion.

5...To serve. Place the salad garnish in the centre of the plate. Slice the hot smoked chicken breasts lengthways and fan around the plate. Spoon the black olive dressing between the slices of chicken. Garnish with tomato concasse and chopped chives. Serves 2 people.

From the menu of...

THE PAINSWICK HOTEL
Kemps Lane, Painswick, Glos GL6 6YB.   Tel: 01452 812160 Fax:814059
Proprietors: Helene and Somerset Moore
Manageress: Julia Robb
Chef: Calum Williamson
Open: All year for lunches and dinner.
Booking advised but casual callers welcome. Children welcome. Credit cards accepted.
Log fires in Winter and outside seating in Summer. Vegetarian and game dishes. Seafood from their own seawater tank a speciality.

Penne Alla Gianni

A quick and simple dish for four people

12oz-350gm dry pasta tubes
2oz-50gm parmesan cheese
7oz-200gm chicken pieces (de-boned)
7oz-200gm mushrooms
3½ oz-100gm mozzarella cheese
1lb-500gm blended tomatoes
¼pt-150ml dry white wine
¼pt-150ml double cream
1 tbls butter

1...Place the pasta tubes in a saucepan of salted boiling water.
2...In another saucepan place the butter and bring to near burning then add the chicken pieces. Turn the heat down and gently saute the chicken until golden brown. Now add the sliced mushrooms and let them also saute for a minute or so. The dry white wine and the blended tomatoes can now be added. Allow the sauce to reach boiling point then add the double cream, mozzarella cheese and parmesan cheese. Stir the sauce to disperse the cheeses.
3...Drain the pasta and pour over the chicken in sauce. Serve immediately.

From the menu of...

GIANNI RISTORANTE
30 Castle Street, Cirencester, Glos.   Tel: 01285 643133
Proprietors: Mr B Sylvestri and Mr B Brizzi
Open: All year. Lunch 12noon-2pm and Dinner 7pm-12pm
Booking advised but casual callers and children welcome. Credit cards accepted.
Outside seating in Summer. Vegetarian dishes. Homemade Italian food and sweets a speciality.

The Traditional Butcher

The traditional butcher is almost as rare as a flock of Cotswold sheep or a herd of Gloucester Cattle. Like thousand of small shopkeepers they have been pushed out of the way by the Supermarket. The difference between the traditional butcher and the Supermarket is that he gives his customer the meat they want while the Supermarket for the customer what they want.

The traditional butcher has had to change to keep in the fray (much to the delight of the specialist farmer.) Supermarket meat is largely mass produced while the traditional butcher buys his meat from small dedicated farmers, many of them working within the boundaries of high organic standards where the welfare of the individual animal is all important and treated with respect. Often the traditional butcher and the farmer of rare breeds work together, and will sell meat by name, Gloucester Old Spot, or Tamworth Pig or Soay sheep, Ruby Red beef, Bronze turkeys and so on.

The surprising thing about the traditional butcher is that he might refuse to sell you meat even though he has it in stock! This is the sign of a truly dedicated butcher. For the best flavour meat should not be sold as fresh as it is in the supermarket. Here it is slaughtered one day, packed and on the shelves less than two days later. For optimum flavour meat should be hung for a minimum of seven days after it has been slaughtered. The reason for this is to develop the flavour and relax the meat. During this time the enzymes in the meat begin to break down the flesh thus naturally tenderising it. There is a disadvantage to the butcher treating meat this way. He has to invest in meat in which he isn't going to get an immediate return and he ha to keep enough storage space to hang the meat which can put a strain on his finances. The advantage is that he can boast to selling the best meat in the area, far better than any supermarket.

Unfortunately, not everyone can afford to buy such superlative meat. You can attempt to emulate the process of hanging by buying meat from the supermarket 5 or 6 days before you intend to eat it (if you have time to think or indeed plan that far ahead). Take the meat out of its plastic wrap. Put it in a container that will fit in the fridge and loosely cover with a clean tea-cloth. This is a poor substitute because of course the traditional butcher does more than just hang meat. He exercises excellent buying skills and can prepare meat any which way you want.

One such butcher in this area is Tetbury Traditional Meats. Like any good traditional butcher they produce their own recipe sausages, their own pies, and cure their own hams. And breakfast will never be the same after you have tried their bacon.

Puddings
and
Desserts

Tastes in puddings vary considerably. Some prefer something cool and refreshing or juicy and fruity and others prefer to indulge in something rich and gooey or creamy and moussy.

Choice of dessert is best dependent on what has gone before. Serve something light if the main meal has been rich and vice-versa. Avoid serving pastry or cream if either of these two ingredients have been involved in the starter or main dish. And again, avoid a fruit pudding if fruit has been involved in an earlier dish. These simple rules will ensure a balanced and interesting meal.

Apple and Blackberry Sorbet

A simple dish to serve either between courses or as a refreshing dessert after a robust Autumn dinner.

1 large cooking apple
8oz-225gm blackberries
8oz-225gm granulated sugar
½pt-275ml water
1 tspn lemon juice
2 egg whites

1...Put the sugar and water in a saucepan. Heat gently until the sugar dissolves then boil rapidly for 8 minutes.
2...Peel, core and slice the apple. Wash and dry the blackberries. Add the sugar syrup and simmer the fruit until the apple has collapsed.
3...Blend the fruit to a smooth puree and pass through a fine sieve. Return the fruit puree to a clean sauce pan and bring to the boil. Boil for 5 minutes
4...Meanwhile put the egg whites in a clean bowl and whisk to soft peaks. While the beaters are still turning slowly pour in the boiling fruit puree. Continue beating until the mixture bulks out and cools.
5...Pour into a plastic container and place on the lid. When the mixture is almost cold put in the freezer and freeze on high for at least 10 hours.

Self Pick Farms

What a wonderful concept the self-pick farm was. In its early days there was a clamour of excited voices praising the farms who opened their gates to the general public so that they could search among the brown earth rows for a choice cabbage, the best beans, the finest fruits... Customers could experience the thrill of picking something straight from the ground without having to grow it first. But the greatest advantage of all was the value, everything was cheaper, not only cheaper than the shops but cheaper than growing it yourself.

The emphasis on the self-pick expedition has changed slightly and is now more often than not considered part of a family day out. There are few simple, inexpensive pleasures left, yet to be out in the warm English sun harvesting a punnet of ripe juicy strawberries or perhaps ruby red raspberries, maybe both, knowing that you will soon be consuming them with some real dairy ice cream or perhaps a spoonful of thick, buttery, clotted cream.

If you are picking quantities to make jam, why not take the whole family and have a competition, who can pick the most in the shortest time, or who picks the best looking punnet, the prize? the biggest dish of strawberries for tea.

In some instances the Farm Shop has become a by-product of the self-pick farm. Here you can buy for a small extra premium, the freshly gathered crops already picked for you.

Farm Shops have developed considerably over the years. A lot of fun can be gained by venturing down dusty farm tracks in search of these, often barn converted, shops. A chance to see the workings of the farmyard and often a delight for children if the is some livestock to see - and much more than vegetables can now be bought. Many farms have gone into producing their own ice-creams, yogurts, sausages, jams and much, much, more, from the produce and livestock on their farm.

Upside-down Apple and Cider Tart

½pt-275ml sweet cider
5 cox dessert apples
4oz-110gm castor sugar
2oz-50gm butter
finely grated rind of half a lemon

3oz-75gm plain flour
3oz-75gm ground almonds
4oz-110gm butter
1 tbls icing sugar
pinch of salt
1 small beaten egg

1...Peel the apples. Cut into quarters and remove the core. Cover and put to one side.

2...In a shallow, metal, saute or frying pan (must have a metal handle) put the butter and sugar. Place over a gentle heat until the butter has melted and the sugar dissolved. Raise the heat and cook until the sugar and butter begins to turn golden. Now add the cider. The mixture will bubble up. Lower the heat slightly and simmer until the sauce reduces by half.

3...Add the apples and lemon rind and simmer for five minutes until the apples are coated and golden. Move the apples around the pan to form a pattern. Put to one side.

4...Mix the flour and ground almonds together and rub in the butter. When you have fine bread crumbs add the icing sugar.

5...Beat the egg and use to bind the mixture together. Rest the pastry for 20 minutes in the fridge.

6...Roll out the pastry to about an inch larger than the pan. Lay the pastry on top of the apples and tuck the edges in.

7...Bake in a pre-heated oven. 220c/425f/gas7 for 25-30 minutes. Remove from the oven and turn upside down immediately onto its serving plate. But do not remove the pan. Let stand in a warm place for twenty minutes. Serve warm with whipped cream that has been dredged with molasses sugar. Serves 4.

Gloucester Pancakes layered with Sautéd Cirencester Orchard Apples, Complimented by a Duet of Cotswold Honey Ice Cream and Elderflower Sorbet

Raechel Harris entered this recipe for the 'Glorious Gloucester Recipe & Cooking Competition'

pancakes:
9oz-250gm self-raising Flour
2½oz-60gm castor sugar
3 eggs
7fl oz-200ml milk
zest of one lemon
honey ice cream:
11fl oz-300ml double cream
11fl oz-300ml milk
4oz-110gm Tetbury honey
4 egg yolks
½ vanilla pod
elderflower sorbet:
11fl oz-300ml sugar syrup, 11fl oz-300ml elderflower cordial,
lemon juice
other ingredients:
4 Cirencester orchard apples
2oz-50gm butter
1oz-25gm sugar
4 sprigs mint
handful of different berries
4 choux lattice baskets
4 sweet paste bases

1...First make the ice cream. Place the cream and milk in a saucepan with the vanilla pod. Bring to the boil.
2...Whisk the egg yolks with the honey until thick and creamy. Pour the boiling liquid into the yolks whisking all the time.
3...Return the mix to the saucepan and heat gently until the custard mixture begins to thicken. Stirring continuously. Do not over heat otherwise the custard will curdle.
4...Strain the custard and cool. When cold pour into the ice-cream machine and churn until ready. Freeze.

5...Now the Sorbet. Combine all the ingredients. (The sugar syrup is made by boiling together for five minutes 8oz-225gm sugar with 1pt-570ml water.) Place in the ice cream machine and churn until ready. Freeze.

6...Lastly make the pancakes. Place the dry ingredients in a mixing bowl then stir in the milk and eggs. Add the lemon zest then whisk until smooth.

7...Heat a griddle or heavy bottomed frying pan and brush over a little oil. Place small spoonfuls of the pancake mixture in the pan, spread out thinly with the back of your spoon. Cook both sides until golden. Keep warm by layering between greasepoof paper and putting in a warm oven.

8...Prepare the apples. Peel, quarter and core four apples then thinly slice.

9...Melt some butter in a saute pan and lightly saute the slices. Sprinkle with sugar to taste. Keep warm.

10...To assemble the dish. Allow 3 pancakes per person. Place the first pancake in the centre of the plate and carefully arrange some apple slices on top. Place a second pancake over the apples, then more apple slices and the third pancake. Sprinkle the final pancake with icing sugar. Place a scoop of Cotswolds honey ice cream and a quennelle of elderflower sorbet to the side of the assembled pancakes. (Depending on your skills, the ice cream and sorbet may be presented in decorative baskets of your choice. For the competition Raechel used a lattice basket made of choux paste for the ice cream and a little sweet paste base for the sorbet.)

11...Garnish with a scattering of local berries and sprig of mint.

From the kitchen of...

THE CLOSE HOTEL
and Restaurant
Long Street, Tetbury, Glos GL8 8AQ.   Tel:01666 502272
Proprietors: Passport Hotels ltd
Managed by: Virgin Hotels ltd
Chef: Paul Welch and team
Open: All year
Uses fresh local ingredients that promote regional dishes and produce.

Gooseberry and Elderflower Crush

Measurements don't have to be strictly accurate for this very simple dessert. When gathering your elderflowers choose umbels that have only just opened.

1lb-450gm gooseberries
4 or 5 heads (umbels) of elderflowers
4oz-110gm castor sugar
4 or 5 broken meringue shells
1pt-570ml double cream

1...Wash and then top and tail the gooseberries. Place in a saucepan with the sugar and elderflowers. Add about 3 tbls water. Cover and simmer gently until the gooseberries are tender and the sugar has dissolved. Stand until cold.
2...Remove the elderflowers heads from the gooseberries (don't worry if a few petals get left behind).
3...Put the gooseberries with the cream in either 1)a blender for a smooth mixture 2) a mixer for a more textured mixture. Blend or beat together until the mixture thickens. Add more cream if too runny. (Be careful not to over beat)
4...Fold in the roughly broken meringues. Spoon into glass dishes and serve with hazelnut shortbread.
Serves 4-6.

Chocolate Roulade

A light and moist dessert which contains no flour. You need best quality chocolate to be special.

The recipe calls for vanilla sugar. Carolyn stores sugar with 6 vanilla pods so that she has a regular supply.

6oz-175gm menier plain chocolate
2½fl oz water
5 large free range eggs
6oz-175gm vanilla sugar
½pt-275ml double cream
1-2tbls cointreau

1...Pre-heat the oven to 200c/400f/gas6 and grease and line a swiss roll tin.
2...Break up the chocolate and put in a basin with the water over a saucepan of simmering water. heat until the chocolate has melted into the water. Cool slightly.
3...Separate the eggs and whisk the yolks with the sugar until pale and creamy. Whisk in the cooled chocolate mixture.
4...Whisk the egg whites until stiff. Fold into the chocolate mixture and lightly spread into the prepared swiss roll tin.
5...Bake until risen in the pre-heated oven for about 20 minutes. Cool.
6...Place a sheet of greaseproof paper on your worktop. Dust the paper liberally with icing sugar. Carefully invert the roulade onto this paper. Peel off the lining.
7...Sprinkle the roulade with cointreau. Whip up the double cream and spread over the roulade. Use the underneath sheet of paper to help you roll it up. Serve in thick slices.

From the kitchen of...

MAD HATTERS
Cafe and Bistro
3 Market Street, Nailsworth Glos GL6 0BX   Tel: 01453 833787
Proprietor/Chef: Michael and Carolyn Findlay
Open: Mon,Tues, Thurs 8.30-5.30. Fri and Sat 8.30-2.30 then from 7pm for dinner. Sunday Lunch from 12.30. Closed all day Wednesday.
Casual callers and children welcome. High chair. Wheelchair access. Informal setting.
Seasonal food and an individual style of cooking. Use organic foods wherever possible and boycott ant food that has involved cruelty to animals. Insist on quality ingredients.

Afternoon Tea

Afternoon tea abounds in the delightful villages of the Cotswolds. From three thirty onwards tearooms and cafes are filled with the mellifluous sound of teaspoons tinkling against the side of tea cups; and the gentle consumption of home-made cakes, freshly baked scones and little dishes of cream, heralds a satisfying end to a fun filled day.

Let's Bake a Cake

It is a great sadness that the weekly tradition of baking a cake has drifted away. Yet the large display of cakes on supermarket shelves and the number of cake shops and patisseries around, and, the number of people who frequent local tea-rooms for a cup of tea and a piece of cake, suggests the tradition of eating cake is very much with us.

Lack of time, for so many women, the usual baker of cakes, is probably the main reason for the demise of the home-baked cake.

Cake is often viewed as something special, a marker for a that personal event like a birthday, a wedding, a christening, a retirement or an anniversary. Also, universally it is made to represent religious festivals such as Christmas and Easter.

Cake making isn't at all difficult, in fact it is difficult to go wrong, provided you follow the instructions to the letter. The most important rule is, always measure your ingredients. Unless you make cakes on a regular basis, (and even then lack of concentration can result in a flop) don't be tempted to guess the measurements. The smallest discrepancy can give imperfect results. Secondly, cake mixtures should be treated with respect. The aim is to get as much air into the mixture as possible, then keep it there. In other words once the beating, whisking or creaming is complete the dry ingredients should be carefully folded in.

Here are a few extra tips. 1. Use soft margarine or make sure the butter is *very* soft. 2. Have the ingredients at room temperature not straight out of the fridge. 3. Use self raising flour. 4. Size 2 eggs are best. 5. Don't bake in too hot an oven.

Cake Making Methods.

Rubbing In: Normally used for fruit cakes. The flour and butter is rubbed together into fine breadcrumbs, the fruit, eggs etc are then added.

Whisking: Swiss roll and gateau sponges. Usually fatless. The eggs and sugar are whisked over the saucepan of hot water until trebled in volume. The flour is very carefully folded in.

Creaming: Victoria Sponge, and the most popular method of cake making. Fat and sugar is beaten together until light and fluffy. Then the eggs are gradually beaten in. The flour is carefully folded in at the end.

Melting: Gingerbread. Butter, sugar, syrup and liquid are melted together with the fruit, cooled slightly, then the flour is stirred in to make a batter.

81

Apple Cake with a Difference

For an extra treat serve with clotted cream.

2lb-900gm Cox's apples
4 tbls elderflower cordial
8oz-225gm margarine or butter
8oz-225gm castor sugar
8oz-225gm self raising flour
4 eggs

1...Peel, core and roughly chop the apples into a large pie dish.
2...Carefully pour the elderflower cordial over the apples so that they are all coated.
3...Cream together the butter and sugar until they are soft, light and fluffy.
4...Whisk the eggs and add them a little at a time to the creamed butter mixture.
5...Sieve the flour and fold it into the mixture with a light touch.
6...Spoon this mixture over the top of the apples.
7...Place in a pre-heated oven 180c/350f/gas4 for 30-40 minutes until golden and risen.
Serve warm with cream.

Recipe supplied by...

THE BOTTLE GREEN DRINKS COMPANY
Frogmarsh Mills, South Woodchester, Stroud, Glos GL5 5ET   Tel: 01453 872882 F:872188
Partners: Dr C B Morris and Mrs S P Morris
Producers of of a range of delicious cordials · elderflower lemon grass, limeflower and Citrus.
Every Spring pickers gather the fragrant elderflower heads from through out the West Country to
make Elderflower cordial. The fresh elderflowers provide a depth of flavour unequalled!

Rich Marsh Bread Pudding

4 loaves bread, white or brown
1lb-450gm mixed dried fruit
3 cooking apples, cooked and mashed, juice strained off
1 tspn marmalade
1 dssrt spn mixed spice
2 eggs
8oz-225gm margarine, melted
8oz-225gm dark brown sugar
1 tspn black treacle
3 grated carrots
1 small cup cooking sherry

1...Cut the crusts from the bread and discard. Break up the bread and pour over a little hot water. Leave to soak for 1 hour. Squeeze the bread mix until nice and soft.

2...Melt the sugar, margarine and black treacle together and add to the bread.

3...Stir in the dried fruit, marmalade, mashed apple, grated carrots and mixed spice.

4...Beat the eggs and add to the mixture. Finally add the sherry.

5...Turn the mixture into a deepish baking tray. Push down and sprinkle with brown sugar. Bake in the oven180c/350f/gas4 for roughly 1½-2 hours until firm to the touch.

Serve warm or cold with cream or ice cream. Ideal for freezing.

From the kitchen of...

THE JENNY WREN
11 The Street, Bibury, Cirencester, Glos   Tel: 01285 740555
Proprietors: Mr J Kemp
Chefs: Mrs M Chivers
Open: All year Winter 10am - 4pm. Summer 10am-5.30pm. Closed 1 week Christmas.
Casual callers and children welcome. Wheelchair access. Bed & Breakfast. Licensed.
Outside seating in teagarden. Traditional home-cooking. Vegetarian dishes. Full menu all day.

Taste of Glorious Gloucester Competition

The Gloucestershire Development agency along with the help of Whitbreads have introduced this annual competition to promote regional produce and ingredients.

There are three classes which means that just about everyone in the county can enter. The Domestic class is for non-professional cooks but who have a keen interest in cooking and regional produce. There is the under sixteen class where potential junior master chefs can practise their skills. The third class is for the trade. Where chefs from regional restaurants and hotels can pit their skills against each other for the top award.

Each class is split up into courses so the winner of the starter can be different to the winner of the main course or sweet.

For the first round every entrant must submit a recipe and this is judged on content, composition, originality and use of Gloucestershire produce. (Many of these recipes will go into the Glorious Gloucestershire recipe book).

The second round is when the four best recipes are chosen from each category. The categories are split up into starter, fish course, main course and dessert. As yet no actual cooking has taken place. This happens at the 'Great Cook Off'.

Round three, and the day of reckoning and several nervous cooks, who have to put their words into practise. One dish from each category is chosen as the best overall recipe. Along with their prizes the winners recipes are served at the Glorious Gloucester V.I.P prize giving dinner.

The competition is a wonderfully innovative with lots of prizes to encourage interest. An idea that not only helps to serve local producers but to boost moral in British food. Paul Welch, head chef of the Close Hotel entered his team for the competition and walked away with two of the top prizes He was truly impressed with the professionalism of the competition and is already looking for ideas for next years competition.

Sous Nuts
(Crunch and Nut Squares)

1lb-450gm cooking fat
7oz-200gm milk powder
7oz-200gm desiccated coconut
3oz-75gm rice crispies
8oz-225gm sultanas
10oz-275gm icing sugar
a few cherries and strips of angelica chopped

1...Mix thoroughly together all the dry ingredients.
2...Melt the fat over a gentle heat. Do not allow to boil.
3...Pour the melted fat over the dry ingredients and blend well so that all the mixture is coated.
4...Spoon the mixture into two ungreased oblong swiss roll tins and press down.
5...Allow to set in the refrigerator then cut into squares.

From the kitchen of...

ST EDWARDS CAFE
and Tearoom
The Square, Stow-on-the-Wold, Glos GL54 1AB.   Tel 01451 830351
Proprietors/cooks: Mrs J White and Mrs S Hathaway
Open: All year. 9am-5pm. Sunday 10am-5pm.
Children welcome. Log fire.

Gooey Chocolate Brownies

4oz-110gm good quality dark chocolate
8oz-225gm margarine or butter
1lb-450gm soft light brown sugar
4oz-110gm self-raising flour
2 tspn baking powder
4 eggs, beaten
8oz-225gm hazelnuts or walnuts

1...Prepare an oblong cake tin by lining it with non-stick parchment.
1...In a large saucepan melt together the chocolate and margarine/butter.
2...When melted add the brown sugar, self-raising flour, baking powder and the beaten eggs. Beat well for 3-4 minutes.
3...Add the nuts then turn the mixture into the prepared tin. Bake in a slowish oven 180c/350f/gas4 for 45 minutes or until crisp on top and gooey in the middle. Allow to cool before cutting into squares.
Delicious served warm with ice cream.

From the menu of...

Crab Apple and Elderflower Jelly

Fruit jellies should be bright and clear, therefore, patience is required. They require a high pectin content and most wild fruits do have this. The amount of sugar required depends upon the amount of juice extracted from the cooked fruit.

4lb-1.8kg crab apples
3 pts-1.75ml water
6 elderflower heads
sugar (1lb-450gm sugar per pint of fruit juice)

1...Wash the fruit and roughly chop. Leave on the peel but remove any brown damaged bits.
2...Put the crab apples and water in a preserving pan and simmer slowly for about 1 hour until the fruit has cooked to a pulp and the liquid has reduced by approximately one third.
3...Set up your jelly bag with clean bowl underneath. Pour in the fruit pulp and leave to strain over night. It is absolutely essential that you don't squeeze the jelly bag otherwise the juice will become cloudy.
4...Measure the juice and the appropriate amount of preserving sugar. Put into a clean preserving pan with the elderflowers. Bring gently to the boil stirring all the time until the sugar has dissolved. Now boil rapidly for 10-12 minutes or until setting point is reached. Take the pan off the heat remove the scum and elderflowers. Pour into sterilised jars while still hot. Seal immediately and leave to set.

To test setting point. a) put a dessert spoon of the jelly on a cold sauce and put in the fridge for 5 minutes. Remove from the fridge and push your finger against the jelly. If thick ripples form it is ready to bottle.
b) Use a sugar thermometer and when 103c is reached the jelly is ready.

Straight From the Bottle

A variety of refreshing drinks and light desserts can be made quickly and simply by using Bottle Green's Elderflower Cordial.

Presse
Add one part cordial to twelve parts of chilled sparkling spring water to make a delicious refreshing drink.

Gin Cocktail
To make this wonderful gin based cocktail, simply add a dash of elderflower cordial to a gin and tonic. Also a dash added to white wine and soda creates a delicious summer cooler!

Ice Cream Soda
Ice cream soda is easily made by measuring 3 fl oz of elderflower cordial to one bottle of soda water and 2 scoops of vanilla ice cream - the children love it!

Ice Lollies
Another favourite with children is made by mixing one part elderflower cordial to five parts spring water and freezing. Delicious ice lollies for those hot summer days.

Fresh Fruit
Pour a little elderflower cordial over the top of fresh fruit salad for a delicious and simple dish.

Ideas from…

THE BOTTLE GREEN DRINKS COMPANY
Frogmarsh Mills, South Woodchester, Stroud, Glos GL5 5ET.
Tel: 01453 872882 Fax: 01453 872188

Towns and Villages

Bibury. No trip to the Cotswolds is complete without a trip to Bibury. It is amazing that this village has managed to preserve its beauty and charm. Set deep in the Cotswolds it is classed as the prettiest village in England. This ancient village still has good evidence of an iron age hill fort and long barrow. The Colne river is an added charm as it winds through the village as is the typical village setting around the church and the pretty cottage gardens. For visitors there is Bibury Trout farm where they can catch healthy rainbow trout; and Arlington Mill Folk Museum. ** Jenny Wren **

Birdlip. A tiny hamlet that can be found on a tiny road outside Stroud in the direction of Cheltenham. ** Kingshead House Restaurant **

Cheltenham Spa. Pigeons are in Cheltenham Spa's coat of arms in reverence to the prosperity their discovery bought to Cheltenham in the early eighteenth century. It is said that they discovered the mineral rich waters in a spring in a meadow outside what was then a little town. The Spa waters put Cheltenham on the map and since then it has developed slowly and carefully into an elegant indeed beautiful town. The town sits neatly on a wide terrace under the great bluff of Cleeve Hill. Delightful flower beds amid wide greens, graceful Regency buildings amid thousands of leafy trees and avenues and fashionable designer shops add up to town that is a pleasure to visit.
** Le Champignon Sauvage ** The Gloucester Sausage Company **

Cirencester. Despite modern intervention Cirencester still manages to maintain of its old crafts. In Medieval times it was the centre of the Wool Trade and probably the reason for its commercialism today. Look hard amongst the modern buildings and you will discover Cirencester Parish church with its peal of twelve bells; the Corinium museum and its Roman collection; the Weavers hall and the Norman gatehouse in Grove Lane. A more traditional atmosphere is captured in the market square amongst the stall holders.
** Gastromania - A passion for Food ** Bomfords Delicatessen **
** The Mad Hatter Wine Bar ** Gianni Ristorante **

Minchinhampton. This medieval parish was closely involved with the development of the wool and latterly the cloth industry. Built in the traditional Cotswold style the market square boasts an interesting Market House elevated on stone columns. In the town is a Queen Ann post office, but today Minchinhampton is probably more well know for its Royal inhabitant Princess Anne. ** The Coffee Bean ** Burleigh Court Hotel **

Nailsworth. This small town is indicative of the wool and weaving industry that was the mainstay of the Cotswolds. It's clock tower and steep narrow streets winding between old mill houses and weavers cottages tells its own tale. Many of the now redundant mills have been brought back to life by the locals and small modern cottage industries are back. It holds an attraction to artists of all types who perhaps see as much beauty in a down to earth country town as in a picturesque country village. ** Tubby's at the Waterfront ** Ruskin Mill Coffee Shop ** The Cookery Nook** Waterman's Restaurant ** Mad Hatter's Cafe/Bistro ** Selsley Herb Shop **

Painswick. Once a market town but now a small village. It is famous for its interwoven avenue of 99 yew trees (the hundredth wouldn't grow, it was said to be killed off by the devil). Custom has enforced a clipping ceremony on the first Sunday after the 19th September. An open air service is held and a Clipping Hymn sung for the event. Lovers of panoramic views should go to Painswick Beacon which overlooks 250 acres of common land, Gloucester and the Severn valley.
* Chancellors at Painswick ** The Country Elephant ** Painswick Hotel *

Stow-on-the-Wold. In May and October the Stow Horse Fair is held although traditionally it was a sheep fair. A nostalgic country fair that is a must for visitors. Around its market square are a good selection of teashops and pubs and offers an beguiling atmosphere.
** St Edwards Cafe and Tearoom ** The Wholefood Shop **

Stroud. As is essential for all mill towns Stroud too is built on a river - the spur of the river Frome. Once the cloth making centre of the West of England it now has only two surviving cloth making mills out of as many as 150 in its hay-day. Today there are still strong symbols that show it was once a busy working town. The old meat market, the Shambles still exists but has diversified into other trades. For anyone interested in the history of Englands early industries a visit to Stroud is a must.
** The Bottle Green Drinks Co ** Mills Cafe ** Edgemoor Inn **

Tetbury. This quiet unaffected towns biggest attraction was once the Woolsack races on Spring Bank holiday Monday. The winner of the race will be the first to man to carry a 48lb sack of wool to the top of Gumstool Hill. This 17th century tradition was revived in 1972 and a street fair accompanies the event. Today Tetbury can boast a far more superior attraction as it is home town for Prince Charles the Prince of Wales who bought Highgrove house when he married Princess Diana.
** The House of Cheese ** The Close Hotel and Restaurant **

Thornbury and ** Thornbury Castle ** are more or less one and the same thing. The Tudor castle has its own vineyard set in 15 acres.

Index of Contributors

Cafes and Tearooms

14 Chancellors at Painswick. Painswick. Tel: 01425 812458
79 Mad Hatters Cafe/Bistro. Nailsworth. Tel: 01453 833787
32 Mills Cafe. Stroud. Tel: 01453 752222
25 Ruskin Mill Coffee Shop. Nailsworth. Tel: 01453 832571
85 St Edwards Cafe. Stow-on-the-Wold. Tel: 01451 830351
54 The Coffee Bean. Minchinhampton. Tel: 01453 883382
86 Tubby's at the Waterfront. Nailsworth. Tel: 01453 834624

Caterers

Entries welcome for next edition

Public Houses, Country Inns and Wine Bars

37 Edgemoor Inn. Stroud. Tel: 01452 813576
68 The Mad Hatter Wine Bar. Cirencester. Tel: 01285 642371

Note to Businesses
If you cook your own speciality dishes,
or if you run a speciality shop,
or sell or manufacture a local product or ingredient
and would like to be featured in the next edition
of this book, please contact
Travelling Gourmet Publications

Producers, Suppliers and Delicatessens

40 Bomfords Delicatessen. Cirencester. Tel: 01285 656900
82 Bottle Green Drinks Co. Stroud. Tel: 01453 872882
22 Gastromania. A Passion for Food. Cirencester. Tel: 01285 644611
25 Ruskin Mill. Nailsworth. Tel: 01453 832571
35 Selsley Herbs. Selsley. Tel: 01453 766682
71 Tetbury Traditional Meats. Tetbury. Tel: 01666 502865
34 The House of Cheese. Tetbury. Tel: 01666 502865
38 The Gloucester Sausage Company. Cheltenham. Tel:01242 680770
36 The Wholefood Shop. Stow-on-the-Wold. Tel: 01451 832194

Restaurants/Bistros/Brasseries

24 Burleigh Court Hotel. Minchinhampton. Tel: 01453 883804
70 Gianni Ristorante. Cirencester. Tel: 01285 643133
18 Kingshead House Restaurant. Birdlip. Tel: 01452 862299
26 Le Champignon Sauvage. Cheltenham. Tel: 01242 573449
69 Painswick Hotel. Painswick. Tel: 01452 812160
46 Thornbury Castle. Thornbury. Tel: 01454 282282
17 The Close Hotel. Tetbury. Tel: 01666 502272
56 The Cookery Nook. Nailsworth. Tel: 01453 832615
21 The Country Elephant. Painswick. Tel: 01425 813564
12 The Jenny Wren. Bibury. Tel: 01285 740555
64 Waterman's Restaurant. Nailsworth. Tel: 01453 832808

92

Conversion Tables

All these are *approximate* conversions which have either been rounded up or down. In a few recipes it has been necessary to modify them very slightly. Never mix metric and imperial measurements in one recipe; stick to one system or the other

WEIGHTS

$\frac{1}{2}$ oz	10 g
1	25
1$\frac{1}{2}$	40
2	50
3	75
4	110
5	150
6	175
7	200
8	225
9	250
10	275
12	350
13	375
14	400
15	425
1 lb	450
1$\frac{1}{4}$	550
1$\frac{1}{2}$	700
2	900
3	1.4kg
4	1.8
5	2.3

VOLUME

1 fl oz	25 ml
2	50
3	75
5 ($\frac{1}{4}$ pint)	150
10 ($\frac{1}{2}$)	275
15 ($\frac{3}{4}$)	400
1 (pint)	570
1$\frac{1}{4}$	700
1$\frac{1}{2}$	900
1$\frac{3}{4}$	1 litre
2	1.1
2$\frac{1}{4}$	1.3
2$\frac{1}{2}$	1.4
2$\frac{3}{4}$	1.6
3	1.75
3$\frac{1}{4}$	1.8
3$\frac{1}{2}$	2.0
3$\frac{3}{4}$	2.1
4	2.3
5	2.8
6	3.4
7	4.0
8 (1 gal)	4.5

MEASUREMENTS

$\frac{1}{4}$ inch	0.5 cm
$\frac{1}{2}$	1.0
1	2.5
2	5.0
3	7.5
4	10.0
6	15.0
7	18.0
8	20.5
9	23.0
11	28.0
12	30.5

OVEN TEMPERATURE

Mark 1	275°F	140°C
2	300	150
3	325	170
4	350	180
5	375	190
6	400	200
7	425	220
8	450	230
9	475	240

Index of Recipes

Mushroom and hazelnut strudel with mushroom sauce 32
Mushroom, savoury pyramid 24

Parsnip and cheese roast 37
Penne Alla Gianni 70
Pesto sauce 28
Pike, Gloucester, and potato cakes with tomato and basil hollandaise 48
Pork with capers and paprika 52
Poussin au Diablo 68

Rich Marsh bread pudding 83
Roasted vegetables topped with grilled goats cheese 30

Sage and onion pork chop 54
Salmon, baked, with ginger sauce 45
Sauces
        Cider butter 21
        Mushroom sauce 33
        Basil 46
        Tomato and basil hollandaise 48
        Ginger sauce 45
        Lemon, mint and soured cream sauce 61
Scallops coated in brioche crumbs and smoked bacon with a caper and
                              gherkin vinaigrette 41
Smoked trout pate 25
Soup
        Wholesome vegetable 12
        Split pea and potato 14
Sous nuts 85

Tenderloin old spot pork, roasted, with woodland mushrooms
                          and tomato 58
Tomato tart, hot 18

Upside down apple and cider tart 75

Watercress tartlets with Gloucester sauce 16
William Pear stuffed with north Cerney cheese 17
Woodpigeon, spiced, with beetroot, barley risotto, chocolate jus 66

Angela Hewitt has been interested in food all her life. Her love of good food stems from her early childhood when she lived with her Aunt and Uncle. They used to run a home-cooked meat and pie shop. Her aunt was a brilliant cook of traditional British food and the table was always plied with good home baking, fresh vegetables, delicious roasts and tasty, natural flavoured stews, with not a stock cube or frozen pea in sight.

For eighteen years Angela was involved in the catering business before taking up food and travel writing.

She started off cooking in a small guest house before taking up the catering concessions at 2 Island yacht clubs.

She opened her own restaurant 'Lugleys' in Lugley Street on the Isle of Wight in 1980. Within a year her cooking was being recommended by Egon Ronay's good food guide. Soon she was in all of the guides and was awarded 2 rosettes by the AA Good Restaurant Guide.

After 14 yrs of anti-social and very tiring hours she decided on a career change in the hope of discovering a more relaxing life style. Since then she has written several regional cookery books, magazine articles and made radio and TV appearances.

Her main interest is in regional and British food and home cooking and how it is changing and affecting people with the influences of foreign imports. The best people to ask she realised, were those people doing it. The food producers, and cooks of each region. So the 'What's Cooking' series was born.

The books are not meant to be a critique but a celebration of food in all its guises. There is a place for everything, and although she is a firm believer of real cooking and the use of fresh and local produce she also knows caterers have to make a living and that the ideal is not always possible and indeed not a true reflection of what is happening on the local food scene.

Whether it is fast food or gourmet food there is a place for it all.

The 'What's Cooking' series is aiming to give a balanced look at food and sometimes to redress the balance when extremes arise.